UND...
HEART

UNDIVIDED HEART

Finding Meaning and Motivation in Christ

LUCY MILLS

DARTON·LONGMAN+TODD

First published in 2017 by
Darton, Longman and Todd Ltd
1 Spencer Court
140–142 Wandsworth High Street
London SW18 4JJ

ISBN 978-0-232-53323-1

A catalogue record for this book is available from the British Library.

Designed and phototypeset by Judy Linard
Printed and bound in Great Britain by Bell & Bain, Glasgow

For Andy
who always believed there would be a 'next one'

Contents

Introduction

Teach me your way, Lord,
that I may rely on your faithfulness;
give me an undivided heart,
that I may fear your name.
Psalm 86:11 (NIV)

We've only just met.

What do I say? How do I explain myself to you, in one easy statement?

My life is full of secrets; even I don't know them all.

Am I the actions I take? The words I use? The labels I wear? It took me over 30 years to feel even somewhat comfortable in my own skin. There are those who seem so sure, aren't there? Not like me, cobbling together the pieces of my identity, trying to locate this elusive 'real me' that people imply should be in here, somewhere.

Can I present you with a set of categories to help you understand me better? What about the bits that I can't define? There are stories within me I'm not ready to tell you, yet they are intrinsic to who I am. You don't see where the sharp edges of life have pierced my heart; you don't know the longings that I hide from view. But these shape and direct my life.

Maybe some of those who look so certain on the outside are just as confused on the inside. Maybe we are all in a constant state of assembling and reassembling the fragments of ourselves. Is there a glue that sticks better than others? An adhesive that really works?

We love to compartmentalise our lives, to make them more manageable – or perhaps to avoid noticing all the conflict that lies within us. Is there a wholeness of purpose and identity that supersedes all the rest, so that we're not left trying to join up the pieces of our lives with dishevelled bits of sticky tape?

We are tugged in all kinds of directions. Our loyalties shift; our eyes slide. We are confused by the times when suffering stalks the goodhearted, when blessing is veiled, when the scriptures of our faith won't be pinned down. We swing between elation at God's revealing and heartbreak at God's hiding. We're told of our identity in Christ, but the words don't always sink in; we hear about the work of the Spirit, but we keep our distance from the One with the power to transform us.

I toddle along in my journey of faith, sometimes satisfying lesser desires but still haunted by that great longing for meaning, for a motivation beyond all the tinny looking 'treasures' that I pick up along the way. It turns out that short-term rewards don't keep me going in the long run; they make my eyes dim; their fuel is not enough. So what reward am I seeking?

I ponder my motives and find them muddled – some well-meaning; some small, dark and selfish. They all pile up together; I look for the beautiful amid the rubbish. Sometimes I catch a glimpse of something worthwhile; other times all I can see is the muddiness of mud.

Give me an undivided heart.

Something in my soul has always been snagged by that phrase in Psalm 86. Something in it speaks to me of my own heart division, my own disarray. It captures a deeper longing, beyond the surface chatter of my mind. I find, amid the muddle that is me, that there is something – *someone* – calling me on, gathering together my disparate, fraying threads and weaving them into a story greater than I could ever perceive.

There are times I've made assumptions about that story; I read the words of the Bible and find I've overwritten it with my own ideas. What does it have to say about what motivates me, about where I find meaning?

Is this you, too? Do you find yourself torn, trying to walk in two directions? Are you uncertain about who you are and why you do the things you do? What are the signposts in your life and which way are they pointing?

You may find, in reading this book, moments of recognition. You may also find yourself challenged to look at something in a different way. Whatever your experience, I hope that these words, these pieces of thought, will be of value to you. Where they are ill-fitting, forgive me. Where they are missing, I pray the divine Spirit will fill the gaps in ways I never could.

Part I
Drives and Desires

Chapter 1
More than survival

*When I look at your heavens, the work of your fingers,
the moon and the stars that you have established;
what are human beings that you are mindful of them,
mortals that you care for them?*
Psalm 8:3-4

I open my eyes. Another day.

I struggle to wake up, to get out of bed. It's not just about moving my body, but mental preparation and emotional effort. I need motivation to engage with the day.

In addition to the side effects of sleeping (drowsiness, the slow computing of my brain), sometimes I'm bombarded by thoughts. Why? Why am I here? Why do I do what I do?

These are the things that toy with my brain, and not just on waking.

My husband sees it coming. I ask questions like, 'When you look at the sky, is your blue the same as my blue?' or 'Aren't hands strange, if you stare at them long enough?' Sure enough, I'm soon having mini-meltdowns at the thought of my existence.

It's one of my many quirks, I suppose.

But some questions are valid. Why *do* I do what I do? What is it that drives me, that propels me through the day? Is it good? Are the things that motivate me the best things of my life?

Or am I stuck too deep inside myself, cornered by fear, perplexity and doubt? What compels me? And to do what?

What am I?
I am human. Of this, I am certain.

My humanity is identified first by how I look: an upright hominid, with rather less hair than most other mammals. I have a face, limbs, a torso – a human body.

But it is, of course, more than that – lying behind these eyes there is a brain full of yet-to-be-explored mysteries, neurones firing...

Thoughts. And not just thoughts but a consciousness of thinking, a consciousness of Being Myself. This astonishes me. I think about thinking, then ponder the fact that I *can* think about thinking.

But as a human, like other creatures, I have one simple drive – to survive.

This is instinct at its most basic. I am alive; I must keep on living. This is not necessarily conscious. I am hungry, therefore I must eat; without food I will die. I am thirsty, so I must drink; without water I will die. I need air to breathe because otherwise I will suffocate; my body will fight to keep breathing. It is designed to eat, to drink, to breathe. If it cannot do these things it will cease to operate. It craves them and I (usually) obey it where I can.

All living creatures need the correct environment and sustenance to exist and to thrive.

I need a world on which to walk.

What else do I need? I need sleep and, in a broader way, rest. Without sleep, my cognitive abilities begin to suffer. I ache; every part of me grows tired.

I need protection from the elements. In some places on this wide earth, lack of shelter would again mean death. I need my immune system to fight germs; I need to escape from danger. I need the *means* to find food, water and shelter. A safe place to live aids my survival, as does good medical care and help from others. Some needs are immediate. Some can be delayed but not indefinitely – without them, eventually, I will cease living. I will not survive.

We humans reproduce, because as individuals we do not keep on surviving. Our bodies betray us; we grow old. Eventually, we break down.

We die.

To survive together – as communities, as a species – we need to work together and take care of one another. When this doesn't happen, the whole community suffers. Survival is not just about what 'I' need, but hinges on our co-operation.

But as a human, I know: we are more complex than this.

Humanity has never been content with just surviving. Once threats to life have been neutralised, we've started building, learning, inventing. On the wider plane of humanity's existence, we've embodied a kind of deliberate evolution – moving ourselves on, exploring, wanting to 'better ourselves' or to make things better for later generations.

Part of humanity's distinctiveness is its ability to adapt to and create multiple environments, its own worlds on which to walk. But these cease to be enough; we plunge on, constantly changing and challenging the perceived norms. Even within a settled society, there are rebels and misfits, those who want to explore different realities, different ways of living.

We want to be creators and explorers, to make and to discover. We want to love and be loved, to know and be known, to understand and be understood.

We are not happy with mere physical survival – perhaps that's where a broader idea of survival comes in. Our basic bodily needs are one thing, but what about our mental, social and emotional needs?

Something 'other'

He has made everything beautiful in its time.
He has also set eternity in the human heart;
yet no one can fathom what God has done
from beginning to end.
Ecclesiastes 3:11 (NIV)

I need more than survival. Is that selfishness? Or does this need come from something deeper, something urging me to look beyond the visible and the temporary to the unseen and eternal?

I need a reason to survive. Something beyond myself, unaffected by my fluctuations of thought and terrors of heart. Something undiluted by the clouds that hover round my mind.

Perhaps this is just another of my quirks. Perhaps.

I need something more than me. I need something more than you or, indeed, all of us together.

I need God.

Some see no need for any kind of 'god' in their lives. Others consider God to be the pinnacle of existence, the main driving force of living – the source of all things, including themselves.

We are not satisfied with our finiteness; there is nothing we create which fully satisfies us, nothing we possess which fully empowers us. Which sounds like a negative thing, but, if you think about it, it is a *high* view of humanity. It recognises that we need something beyond our futilities, something more than ourselves. We may be finite, but we are always stretching our hands out for more.

The apostle Paul quoted that 'in him we live and move and have our being' (Acts 17:28). Underpinning this belief is the idea that if there was no God, there would be no 'us'. The biblical picture is of a God who does not create-and-run, but who continues to sustain creation and uphold our existence.

For a believer, then, God is the primary necessity for survival – for all of life – because without God *there would be no life.*

I believe in God. Sometimes that belief stutters and the void yawns before me, but I get pulled back, again and again. I keep going because of God. God is what I desire most, even when I'm all muddled and confused. I want to know who God is – who God *really* is; I don't want to believe in a character conjured up by myself or by anyone else. I need to be reminded that I don't 'live by bread alone', that God is the source of life.

Not everyone will agree with that, I know, but this belief has formed my life, motivated me to take certain paths and refuse others, made me feel and think in certain ways. I am moulded by this belief. It has made me who I am.

Beyond the blue

The reality of existence is astonishing, our complexity undeniable. But to explain such complexity does not underrate it. Rather, it only shines a light on it, giving us moments of 'wow' – when something tightens in our chests and throats, when our very breath stutters.

I remember spending a birthday weekend at my parents' house. After a meal out with family and local friends, some of us went out into their back garden. On that glorious, unpolluted night, the stars were all clamouring to show themselves. The vast, powdery swathe of the Milky Way glimmered against the blackness. As I stared up into this vast reality, it was as if not only my body staggered but that my soul toppled backwards as it tried to take in the view. I felt tiny and yet so privileged to live, to *see* this, although its hugeness frightened me. My throat constricted.

I had never seen so many stars. I had never felt so small.

Another moment – this time in our own back garden – I was staring up at the day-sky, watching a red kite. As the fork-tailed bird of prey glided across a blue backdrop frothy with cloud, I considered the fact that I was here, in this spot, on this planet. Beyond the blueness was the enormity of space.

Such moments peel away my pettiness, my selfishness – and I am left shuddering with awe.

It makes me think: if I am so awed by the idea of the universe, how am I to begin comprehending the idea of its maker? It does not compute. Neither does it compute that such a maker would take on the feeble flesh I wear as part of my humanity. The idea fizzes: it is too, too big. Or too, too small.

I love such experiences but I'm not sure I could live every moment like that. I would hardly be able to walk from one place to another. I would have to keep crawling to the floor, kneeling – down, down, down or lying face upwards, just staring – up, up, up.

But these moments remind me – survival is not enough. I need more. I look at my divided life, the fragments of my days and I scowl at how I use my time, at how little I look up, up, up or kneel down, down, down.

What really drives my life? How can I be undivided in my pursuit of life, of God? Often I *am* divided – in my motives and intentions, in my focus and my goals, because of fear or doubt or numerous other things. I end up with one foot in and one foot out. I dangle on fences, perch on walls, wave from the edges, not quite able to take the full plunge into the unknown – or even to commit myself to what I already know.

I'm not even sure what's stopping me, most of the time.

The ledge

'Put your foot on the ledge,' they tell me. I've seen others do it, from the bottom of the parish church tower, but now, one shaking leg over the top of the parapet, I can't find the ledge. I'm not abseiling from a cliff; here there's a barrier I need step over in order to continue.

The ledge is down the other side of the wall. It's where I need to put my first foot, then hoist my other leg over to join it before beginning my descent.

'Is it there?' I demand, in the end, because for all my stretching, *I cannot feel the ledge.* Despite having witnessed others stepping onto it, it now seems an impossibility.

A church volunteer looks over the edge. 'You're nearly there,' he tells me. 'Just a little lower.'

Sinking uncomfortably low – remember my other leg is still on the church roof – at last, my foot grazes the ledge. I feel brief exhilaration at its existence, as well as astonishment that it was *so far down.* Then I have to get my other leg over, which proves difficult, as my fluctuating fear of heights makes it jelly-like and uncooperative. I need help to lift my foot.

Once both feet are on the ledge I wait, impatient and trembling, for instruction. Nothing comes.

'Do I just lean back and walk?' I ask.

'Just lean back and walk,' they agree.

I want firmer step-by-step instructions, but it appears that's all I'm getting. They seem bored; they've been doing this for a couple of hours. My fears are same-old, same-old.

This has to be me; I have to decide to walk. I move my hands from the wall to the harness.

Everything changes.

When I lean back, I feel the harness holding me; when I let go of the parapet, my confidence returns. I have to *stop* clinging to the wall in order to feel secure in what I'm doing. My fear dissipates and I enjoy my walk down the wall.

The hardest part? For me, finding that elusive ledge. Locating it gave me what I needed to continue. It was – despite my panic, despite my inability to find it – *there*.

This book is my journey as much as it is yours. I'm digging down, crying out, hoping to change, longing to believe – instead of dithering and doubting, wanting yet not-quite-doing... I'm ready to take my first step, to find that ledge from which I begin. Come with me and we'll see where it leads us. I think we might even enjoy it.

Squinting my eyes
(in what I hope is your direction),
I see a faint light.
I take a breath,
stand up
and start walking.

REFLECT
- What do you think it means to be 'human'?
- Where and when have you been affected by moments of awe?
- Do you struggle to find the starting point – 'the ledge' – in your life of faith?

O God, it puzzles me –
how great you are
and how small I feel.
The vastness of the universe
is far too great to grasp –
let alone the extravagance
of its maker.

O God, turn my thoughts to you
when my life feels full
of obstacles, of busyness,
of metaphorical mountains
I am required to climb
(though I often don't feel dressed
for the occasion).

O God, compassionate creator,
awesome redeemer,
draw near amid my fears,
despite my doubt.
Break through my bewilderment
and call me to follow you
once more.

Chapter 2
Default settings

Everything we experience registers in our being and affects the way we think, act and react, although we may be completely unaware of the reasons for our behaviour.
Gerard W Hughes[1]

How might I describe myself?

I have blonde hair – sort of, at least in summer, when it's caught by the sun. But I've found strands of deep red and dark brown before.

I have grey eyes – sort of, it depends on the light; they can also look blue or green.

I am kind – sort of, apart from those moments when I, to my shame, feel nothing much at all and have to summon the 'correct' response.

I am curious – sort of, until I am in one of my dulled states, when everything ceases to be interesting.

I am loving – sort of, until I'm really hurt and, stung into anger, say (or at least think) something very unloving indeed.

I am 'sort of' many things.

You will have your own 'sort ofs'. You'll also have your own 'definites'.

I'm definite about this: I am the child of my parents. I grew up where I did. I have a nose and two eyes and a mouth.[2] But how much of 'myself' can I break down?

The making of me
What is the default template for 'me'? Is there a Lucy Mills blueprint? Am I driven by my genes? Shaped by my environment? Most would now say: both.

I can't hold my 'personality trait' cards and my 'gene' cards and

---

[1] Gerard W Hughes, *God of Surprises* (Darton, Longman and Todd, 1985)
[2] At the time of writing, anyway.

match them up with ease, like a game of snap. Whatever genetic influence is, it is more complicated than that. There *are* diagnosable genetic disorders which shape people's lives in specific ways. Genes do result in particular attributes, such the colour of my eyes, the shade of my skin, the 'dominant gene' winning the game. But as for all the ingredients which make up 'me' – I would not like to guess. And when we start moving away from physical attributes and into personality, things get harder to define. Yes, in my genes lie the beginnings of the making of me, but there are so many other influencers. Disentangling them is hard indeed.

I'm shaped by my environment, my family background, what I've been taught about the world and about myself, how I've been treated, the friendships I've gained and lost, the way I spend my days.

Each experience challenges the current 'model' of me, as it brings something new to it. I can react against it, absorb it or adapt to it, depending on the nature of the experience and its impact. Is it a one-off, or is it repeated – a new constant I wasn't expecting? Is it destructive or creative? Does it have a soft impact, or is it something soul-shattering? Is it unexpected, or is it an intentional change or new commitment? Is it premeditated or spontaneous? How does it interact with my previous experiences – do I deal with them differently, in the light of it?

> *How many pieces are there*
> *in the story of myself?*
> *How many threads are woven*
> *inside this fragile heart?*
> *How many triggers have there been*
> *leading me here to this moment,*
> *experiencing these symptoms,*
> *asking these questions?*

Consequences

We pick up patterns of behaviour and learn attitudes from others. Sometimes we react against them, especially if they are in an extreme form. Hypocrisy in others can lead us to reject the truth they proclaim because they don't live according to the values they profess. (This, perhaps, is one of the saddest motivators of all – disillusionment created by the actions, or inaction, of other human beings. Even if what they profess is truth, they muddy it in the mind of others. It's become equated with something different – whether it's the role of a parent, an ideology, a community, a belief: *If that's what a Christian is, I want nothing to do with it.*)

I couldn't list all the character-shaping factors in my life. Some I will have forgotten, or never realised the change they made in me. We're not always aware of our prisons nor, conversely, of our freedoms; our reality is our 'normal' and we adapt to it, good or bad. Experience tinkers with our programming, inserting extras into our 'normal' so that the default changes, subtly or not so subtly, into something else. We don't always realise when the template for 'normal' has been changed.

The personal recipe found in my genetic code helps form that 'default' me. I have tendencies toward some things and not others. Should this define me? I suppose we might say, well, it depends if these tendencies are good or bad – and thereby open another can of worms. If something is seen as 'my nature', does that necessarily mean it is good? What if it is in my nature to be cruel? What if I have a tendency towards an ugly kind of jealousy, or like to see other people hurt?

Where there is a genetic tendency, or what we might see as an 'innate gift' for something, the right environment can cause it to flourish, for good or ill. If I have a knack for something, the right place and the right kind of 'nurturing' helps me thrive at it. But if I am easily led or tempted by certain things and find myself in an environment or in company that reinforces my more destructive behaviours, it works the other way round, too.

Nature

A wonderful fact to reflect upon, that every human creature is constituted to be that profound secret and mystery to every other.

Charles Dickens,
in A Tale of Two Cities

Sometimes our defaults are just different. But they can be reinforced, or shifted, by that which we encounter. Even in wider creation, we can see how temperaments differ from creature to creature – and these may be innate, learned or both.

When I was growing up we had two Labradors – one black, one golden. One was buoyant, unafraid, impatient. The other was more easily alarmed and at the same time more inclined to allow you to cuddle up to her if you, too, were finding the world a bit much.

One year we had a snowman in the back garden. Misty, our golden Labrador, stared at it from the lounge window, her whole body stiff and alert. Misty didn't give the short sharp barks uttered by Bonnie, her elder. Misty's cheeks would inflate, her mouth emitting little puffs of air, tiny 'wuffs' hovering, unimpressive and barely audible, until she threw back her head and hollered.

A-wooo-wooo-wooo!

Misty hollered at the snowman.

When we opened the back door, Misty crept through the snow with hackles up. Bonnie romped past her to the snowman, swiped the carrot nose and ate it.

They were *different*.

But it was easy to reinforce the behaviour. When Misty quaked at thunderstorms, I held out my arms and she ran to me. However, we realised this was only confirming her anxieties, so we adjusted our 'technique' by talking cheerfully to her, rather than making her believe there was something to fear.

I liked feeling needed. I liked it when my trembling dog buried herself in my arms. My sympathy was ready to bestow as soon as I heard the first rumble of distant thunder. But it didn't help her overcome her terror. I had to adjust *my* behaviour, based on *my* tendencies, too.

We all have things in our current 'default' that we don't like. Whether these are caused by genetic influence, environmental factors or destabilising circumstances may, in some cases, be moot. We can't trace everything back, define everything in this way. Most of the time it is guesswork.

But it seems reasonable to suggest that if each person has their own specific set of challenges – their own gifts and their own less appealing traits – we can't impose one template on every individual person, just as we can't address all of life's situations in the same way.

The dark side of our hearts

What about the really nasty bits? When something grubby and unpleasant comes out of our hearts? We talk about creation, fall, redemption and renewal; these are ways of making sense of the fracturedness we sense within us. The biblical narrative tells us a story with which we interpret our 'cracked image' – emphasising the goodness of creation and our flaws, too.

'All creation groans' for its redemption; the impact of evil is far-reaching. We read in the story of Noah that 'every inclination of the human heart is evil from childhood'. The Psalmist despairs at the extent of human failure: 'All have turned away, all have become corrupt; there is no one who does good, not even one.' This is later quoted by Paul, who builds on this, saying that 'all have sinned and fall short of the glory of God'.[3]

Is that our intended state? To be 'unrighteous', to be 'far from God'? In the Bible, the words most often used for sin mean 'missing the mark'. We fail to live as God intended, in how we think, speak and act. We 'fall short'; we don't hit the target; our aim is somehow 'off'.

There is a bleakness at the heart of humanity.

And yet –

We strive for life, for hope, for goodness. Goodness not as an insipid, archaic word, but something vibrant, powerful, God-stamped, contagious. Within our striving, we are not alone, for the living breath of God is as real today as when it first breathed into creation. It still brings life; it still puts flesh on dry bones; it still floods parched lands with living water. As we view the divine through our human lenses, we hear hints, whispers. We look to Jesus; we listen to the Spirit; we read the ancient words of inspired, human prophets, who longed for hope and justice in their time, as we do in ours.

Yes, there is something 'off-target' or 'off-key' in the hearts of humanity, but in those same hearts is the extraordinary potential for good, because we were created to be image-bearers.

It is useless to deny the existence of evil in our world; we see it enacted every day. It is useless for me to deny that I have thoughts and impulses of which I am ashamed. I am all too aware of the frequent times I 'miss the mark', either by action or by inaction, not glorifying God but stubbornly prioritising myself and my own 'wants' – or 'not wants'.

To be a Christ follower means seeking a new 'default', shaped by this faith journey and the One I follow, not by what I would be without him. I dread to think what I would be without him. Some people are strong on goodness, morality and kindness.

Most of that stuff I get from Jesus.

Jesus showed us what it means to be human, by being human himself.

For all of us, our current default is the same (all have fallen short) and yet different (we all have our own shapers and markers).

[3] Romans 8:22; Genesis 8:21; Psalm 14:3; Romans 3:23

We are intended to know God; we are intended to give God glory. Our corrupted default settings need not just restoring but upgrading, transforming. We are to be God-focused, not self-focused. We are to mature in faith. We need to be just and compassionate and pure, even when our current default state seems to be a bit lacking in these things.

But there is so much that tugs at us, so many things we crave. How do we deal with our own desires – and how do these affect our behaviour?

> *Search me, O God, and know my heart;*
> *test me and know my thoughts.*
> Psalm 139:23

REFLECT

- What do you consider your 'natural' traits and your 'learned behaviours'?
- What do you wish you could change about yourself?
- What about your life gives glory to God? What falls short?

When face to face with myself,
I feel the contradiction:
On the one hand, I am only one.
I am so small, so dust-like –
a sand speck
on the beaches of the universe.

On the other hand,
I am so complex – to deny that
would be to simplify myself
to such an extent that I never grasp
that I can be different,
that I can change,
that the drivers of my life
do not need to be my dictators.

Help me, maker of my heart,
to have a balanced view of me
and what makes me who I am.

Chapter 3
Wired for desire

Hope deferred makes the heart sick,
but a desire fulfilled is a tree of life.
Proverbs 13:12

It starts small – a prickle of discomfort, a sense of lack. Or it comes on suddenly – fierce, overwhelming. I *want*.

Desire tunes into some of our basic needs: yearning to be warm or safe. Longing to be loved, noticed, wanted. It can be specific – I don't just want food; I want *that kind* of food.

We might want things because they have positive effects on us or those around us. We can crave objects, people, feelings – or other things too abstract to explain. We want romance or adventure or to watch the next episode of our favourite programme. We want to connect with something or someone.

The woven threads of want

Each day holds desires of all kinds. These range from the trivial to the profound, from those impulses you barely notice to something that transforms the whole feel of the day. It might drive you to an action that *alters your whole future.* Such is the varied power of desire.

We have basic cravings and impulses; these may be survival-based or pleasure-orientated. We have more complex desires based on our higher emotions and intellect, our broader plans and hopes. Sometimes, these conflict with our more 'primal' urges. In fact, to meet one desire, we may have to ignore another, as it will get in the way of fulfilling the first. We can't divide our impulses into easy boxes. They interconnect; we don't always see the threads that weave them together.

We can want what we *don't* want and not want what we *do* want. Which sounds nonsensical, but we know it isn't. There are things we don't want to desire. Things that we could do with *not* wanting. We can want two opposing things in different ways.

We recognise that some of our impulses are not good. We

understand Paul's strained statement: 'I do not understand my own actions. For I do not do what I want, but I do the very thing I hate...' (Romans 7:15) These words sum up the agony of the conflict – we want to do good but, on another level, we crave the opposite and that urge is powerful indeed. Even the best of our deeds can come from mixed motives.

We want to be *happy*. The pursuit of happiness is a big thing for us, although how we 'get' it is a matter for debate. What about when our 'happiness' comes at the expense of another's? Desire is often geared towards fulfilled pleasure, or at least satisfaction. Desire *itself* can bring pleasure. Consider the power of anticipation – it's not just about the reward, but knowing that the reward is coming. The unopened present, full of potential to please us, can be pleasure in itself.

The aim of a desire may not be as high as 'happiness'. It may be a wish for distraction from boredom, a way of escaping from oneself. If not seeking happiness, then at least we usually want *not to be sad*.

Competitors

We live in a world in which short-term rewards are constantly on offer, but this can reduce the incentive to chase long-term rewards. We may be conscious of this and get frustrated by our own weakness. But the easy option is, well, *easier*. There's so much available at our fingertips and it's easier to think in 'bitesize'.

I'm reading a book. There's no background noise except the mild humming of the house, the central heating bubbling faintly on this February day, the twittering of starlings muffled by double glazing. I am relishing, in the most part, this glorious peace. I feel *nourished.*

And yet, I'm not completely relaxed. In this deep, slow action of reading a book, I am holding something else in check: the desire to snatch up the nearest device to check and scroll and click and play, *at the expense* of the satisfaction I have in what I am doing now. Every now and then it prickles; I sit on it until it subsides.

Sometimes I win and it stays muffled, squashed by my control. I read another chapter. At other times, I reach a chapter break and it's a great excuse – my mind's eye slides towards my smartphone or my tablet, towards the bright screen. At a profound level I am annoyed by this urge, it's not what I want to do. Yet we are getting so used to short-term gratification, to constant stimulation, that we feel odd without it. It takes discipline *not to look.*

I'm grateful for much that the digital age offers and our increased abilities to connect. But I feel a twitch of regret that I need to hold this desire in check, as it's spoiling my moment. The temptation is there, however faint – I wonder what I would achieve without its clamouring call. Because when I give in and click that button, I am briefly satisfied, but no longer at peace, not *nourished* in the same way. One desire trumped the other, as I opted for a shorter route to satisfaction.[4]

You may not relate to this at all, but there will be other things. What is it that prickles at your mind or body when you are finally allowing yourself to relax? It may not be as inane as a bright screen. It might be something far more exhausting. It could be the temptation to worry away at something. (Can we desire to worry? Perhaps not. But we can begin to worry as our default and feel guilty if we stop, or forget, for a moment, the thing we were worrying about.) We can entertain unhealthy ideas or think nasty thoughts about someone or lust after what we don't have. We might want to prove ourselves to others, or to 'look busy' – so much so that sitting down never feels justified!

There are 'shameful' desires we try and hide. For some the bright screen may be part of that desire – opening up a web of darkness. Perhaps it is all played out inside your own mind and you will later weep at your own thoughts, but struggle to fight them now. Desire can take hold of us in one way and yet not be what we 'want' at a higher level in our brains; we indulge ourselves until we are sick of ourselves, consumed by self-loathing. Yet still we can't let go, because we've entered a cycle – the indulgence now becomes a distraction from the self-loathing it caused.

We no longer have the appetite for over-eating but we can't stop, because stopping would mean seeing what we have become.

I do not do what I want, but I do the very thing I hate...

Thrill me

When something gives us a pleasure reaction, we want more of it. Even if the pleasure itself is not inherently bad, chasing after it repeatedly can make for an unhealthy obsession or even addiction. Is the desire for the thrill dictating your life? Do you feel twitchy when you haven't 'topped up' on it? Do you try to expand it – going for a deeper thrill each time?

[4] This is an example of one desire interrupting another and isn't a statement about technology per se. Further reflection on using digital media is found in chapter 8.

The direction of desire matters. It can be focused on something worthy or good. It can also go wrong, if it is pointed in a harmful direction, hacked into by manipulative or unfriendly hands, or ambushed by the unworthy or the unhealthy or the cruel.

As certain pleasures cease to satisfy, we seek out more extreme ways to please ourselves. This is part of pornography's power. After a while, what you are seeing is not enough. You want more, and it takes you away from a true and beautiful celebration of sexuality. The transition from 'soft' to 'hard' drugs is easier than users initially imagine.

How much begins with the 'I'll just do it the once'?

When the thing you craved does not have the substance or ability to satisfy in the way you hoped, you go on to the next thing, whatever that might be. What once seemed exhilarating now seems boring.

Let's talk about...

One of the strangest contradictions in contemporary Western society surrounds the idea of romantic relationships. On one hand, sexual freedom is promoted and practised; old ideals and traditions seem strange and out of place; abstinence looks odd to many. But then at the same time is this pervasive idea of the One – idealised in so many songs and stories – one wonderful soulmate who would make us happy if only we could find that person and be swept off our feet.

We are led to the (erroneous) conclusion that there is a human being who can provide *all* we want, *all* we need, *all* the time. A relationship that will last – in the same exhilarating way – forever. Until it doesn't. Then we start again.

The portrayal of sex on film and TV can imply that everything always happens as it should do, all things fit exactly as they are supposed to first time and that if they don't, you aren't 'sexually compatible'. Thus there is no hope for your relationship and it is not worth working at it.

In reality, it can be area reeking with insecurity as people worry about meeting other's expectations, unable to match the models put forward by an increasingly sexualised culture. They may even withdraw completely and affect disinterest, rather than feel their partner's perceived disappointment, or disappointment in themselves at not being good enough. As pornography rockets, as more young people and children are exposed to it, as the dark web weaves its spell and makes things more readily available to those who know where to look – our understanding of what sex is, and how it relates to our identity, shifts. Sometimes our identities feel so bound up with it that it becomes a primary marker of who we are. At its best, sex is an expression of love and connectedness but, in a society of short-term stimulation, it is often a place of disconnect.

Custom-made

We're wired for desire, but we're not all wired in the same way. We don't all desire the same things. We don't see the appeal in something another person finds fascinating or difficult to shake off. We don't always understand the influence a thing or activity has over a person (it may *be* another person), but we need to recognise its power.

'Why don't you just…' is rarely a productive or helpful thing to say when we're addressing something which has such a hold. It's not that easy. Exasperation can overpower our compassion, but we must try to resist, otherwise we condemn someone else to a lonely struggle, downplaying the serious impact of their desire.

It's not the same for everyone. But those who find such immediate 'thrills' easy to resist and shrug off need to take care not to dismiss those who find them more compelling. There will be other, different struggles which affect those who come across as 'smug' about certain weaknesses. We mustn't ignore the struggles some have with desire (of whatever kind), whether it is a trivial irritant hampering daily living; a consuming addiction; or something that leads to a lifetime of longing.

Desiring God

> *Every longing we possess is a secret longing for God.*
> *We may accidentally attach this longing to something*
> *or someone else – but only God, whose reflections*
> *and shadows these are, can really satisfy us.*
> Alister McGrath[5]

Our desires are often to do with pleasure and satisfaction, but at their heart there is often a need for connection – a heart-touching-heart scenario, that one day we will be fulfilled. Often in these dreams of fulfilment we are not alone – woven in is the idea of *somebody else* and something bigger than ourselves.

[5] Alister McGrath, *Knowing Christ* (John Murray Press, an imprint of Hodder & Stoughton, 2001)

Desire can be beautiful. Let's not paint it as bad – to *long* for what is worth longing for can be painful but still hold great joy. To have the feelings that we do – to crave, to need, to want, to *care* – these make us who we are, fuelling, at their best, hope and faith and love.

There's something wonderful about the desire to 'connect' with others, the desire to love and be loved, the desire to explore and experience new things, the desire to feel at home, the desire to seek truth or knowledge. The sad thing is when these desires get fogged by cravings for lesser things, not necessarily bad in themselves, but looming large in the foreground. As they consume our vision we may never notice the distant mountain ranges, the astonishing backdrops of our lives, the wonder of the sky in all its guises, all the glorious things we could learn and become.

On my best days, I crave truth and meaning and understanding. These are not easy days; often the desire is jarring, uncomfortable, as I stretch for something I cannot see clearly nor 'prove'.

We can reach so far, in our human wisdom and experience; we can glean so much from reading and studying scripture, relishing new insight, getting deep into context and meaning; we can sense so much in our divine encounters, through the powerful whisper of the Spirit, but there are things we cannot pin down, not yet. There are mysteries still to be revealed, hopes still to be fulfilled, pictures still not painted.

To hunger for the true God is a journey of knowing and unknowing; of thinking you know and then discovering you really, really don't; of suddenly seeing something differently; of being prepared to be wrong in your interpretation or your standpoint; of faith, doubt, sadness, joy, exhilaration, frustration and all things in between.

O God, transform me in all my wanting;
focus my heart on you alone.

REFLECT

- What do you 'want'?
- Are there desires in your life which have an unhealthy hold on you?
- What desires would you like to see in yourself?

Guardian of my heart –
my fingers are aching
from my attempts to play the right notes.

My feet are tired from walking
a path for which my shoes
do not always feel adequate.

I've been busy examining my faith
and wondering if it is big enough –
but of course, faith is not supposed
to look at itself at all, but towards
something else.

Someone who is more than big enough,
greater than all my uncertainty
and weariness.

You sustain me, you alone.

I fix my eyes
not on my fingers or my feet,
not on the pathway
nor the style of my shoes.
I fix my eyes on you –
you who are greater than all these things.

I believe; help my unbelief.

Chapter 4
Sharp edges and broken hearts

Every man has his secret sorrows which the world knows not;
and often times we call a man cold when he is only sad.
Henry Wadsworth Longfellow

As well as things that attract us, there are also things that repel us, sharp edges that make us draw back. They adjust our behaviour (we might wish they didn't). Sometimes we're not even aware of them; sometimes they are *all* we can see.

Warning signs
Fear is natural, even necessary, to our humanity. It has been important to our survival – running from predators, avoiding harmful situations, not getting into that car. It can be wise to be afraid. Lack of fear can make us rush in headlong, regardless of consequences.

But too much stifles us, traps us. We become imprisoned by it, as an agoraphobe cannot leave the house, or unable to do everyday things, like an arachnophobe faced by a spider in the shower. When this happens, fear does not just shape our lives; it dictates them.

Pain, too. Pain is important. It tells us something is wrong, that something has wounded us. Without the ability to feel pain we are injured too readily; we don't know that something is too hot or too sharp; we don't adjust our actions accordingly.

The breaking of skin causes pain – *here.* Here is the wound; this is the source. *Where does it hurt?* is the first stage of a diagnosis. *What kind of pain is it*? often follows. It also affects how we treat the area. We cradle the arm that has been broken. We 'nurse our wounds' because they sting. Pain encourages us to give our bodies what they need to heal. In that sense, it is good for our health.

But some wounds aren't easy to treat or even diagnose. Chronic illness, incurable injury or disease, something faulty in our bodies or brains – these can make pain a constant and dominant reality.

Pain can be a stopping force. As someone with ME/CFS, I have grown accustomed to a certain level of tiredness and pain. (This is both positive and negative – I live in adapted ways, but sometimes I don't obey the warning signs!) It shapes my life. I can make positive and negatives out of this shaping – not all the side effects are bad. God is gracious and brings me blessings in my place of weakness. But that doesn't mean I don't detest it at times and that it doesn't, as a fellow sufferer once put it, make me want to 'throw all my toys out of the pram' on occasion.

What do I say, when someone congratulates me on how well I'm looking, when I feel appalling? When the fatigue bites, I'm too exhausted to explain.

We cannot always see someone else's pain, nor know the things that cause them dread.

I doubt it
Never criticise a man until you've walked a mile in his moccasins.
Native American proverb

Doubt is one of my 'sharp edges'. (It may not be yours, but be gentle with me.)

Some are more inclined towards doubt than others. For some it is cerebral, a worry in their minds. For others, it's a gut-deep uncertainty, an emotional response that is hard to reason away. For some (including me), it's a messy knot of both.

Mother Teresa, who was often hailed as a 'perfect Christian' and canonised by the Catholic Church after her death, confessed in letters to having deep, desperate doubt throughout her life. Some hailed this news with atheistic glee – *What a charlatan!* Others heaved a sigh of relief because, well, they know how she felt.

There are those who shrug their shoulders and claim that doubt has never really been a problem for them. I admit, when faced with these shoulder-shruggers, I feel small and somehow ... less. It's as if there's a flaw in me I can't fix, as if I only tried hard enough, or 'stopped being so silly', or just learned to let go, I could be ... well ... different. I swing between admiration and irritation at those who cannot understand my wobbliness.

Sometimes the worst thing you can say to someone is that something is easy. It dismisses their difficulty. Just as with desire, someone else's sharp edges won't be yours. But that *makes them no less sharp to that person.*

I said in the first chapter that I *need* God, but there are times I *doubt* God. These two conditions make for moments of quiet terror.

To put a lid on doubt, I step back, I disengage. My automated systems carry on, while my heart goes offline. I am, in a deep sense, divided. I long for God and for the freedom to chase after God, but the reality is that just I am about to start running towards God, doubt *sits* on me.

Doubt is heavy, so I get a bit squashed.

> *Teach me Your way, O Lord;*
> *I will walk in Your truth;*
> *Unite my heart to fear Your name.*
> Psalm 86:11 (NKJV)

'Unite my heart!' Some Bible versions use this translation of that line in Psalm 86. I may have been soul-snagged by the phrase 'give me an undivided heart', but I ponder this alternative translation and find it helpful.

Lord, unite my heart. Get rid of the duality within.

I've realised that my doubt is less to do with God than it is to do with me. I doubt my ability to know God; I doubt all human constructs that reach for God. To cope, I do the worst thing possible – I retreat from the One who would help me the most, because I doubt my capacity to hear and respond to that One.

My preoccupation with my own ability to perceive can do something damaging – it makes me look away. I keep second guessing myself, looking *at* my faith rather than looking *with* my faith (two different things, I have discovered).

It divides me, this toxic dissemination, because I don't dare trust myself; I don't trust my ability to know God; I don't trust my mind to comprehend nor my emotions to feel 'correctly'. I divvy myself up into disparate portions. I'm in a perpetual stalemate.

It's a joy stealer.

A deeply-held belief is such a life-shaper, so bound up with identity and loyalty and love. The idea of losing it can be shattering. Our doubt doesn't change God. But it can tie us up, so that even as we walk we are in a constant state of injury. The stones in our shoes cut into our skin every time we take a step.

How to move forward? I'm not sure I know yet. But understanding the problem eases the constriction around my heart.

I trust you, God,
underneath it all;
in a place beyond words
or understanding,
I trust you.

Some may ask: how can you believe in a God who allows such horrors, such atrocities, across the bloody scape of human history, past and present suffering leeching hope from the earth?

I don't know. But in such a world, I cling to God alone.

A heart that craves God, loves God and puts all hope in God *despite* doubt does not oppose intellect – it goes beyond it.

I will not stop seeking this God, even if I bleed for it.

Some might despise me for such an answer. *It's not good enough.* They are scandalised by Christ on the cross, to whom I look in such moments – it's just another appalling act. As if God pointed his finger and said – *DIE.* They don't see a co-operative decision made in the triune heart of a loving God desperate for his children, but an act of a deranged and angry father.

It's not good enough, they may say. It's offensive that I should believe in God at all.

And yet I do. Because it's all I have.

In the darkness, all my babbling doubts are stripped away. In the darkness, of all places, I believe. Because it's all I can do.

It springs from some part of me I cannot see.

Shapers and breakers

Yes, life has sharp edges, the things that pierce us and wear us down, the things that make us limp or run, the things that make us draw away for fear of another painful encounter. They affect how we approach our lives and what we do with them – on both the micro level of daily living and the macro landscape of how our lives progress.

No doubt you can think of your own 'sharp edges', the things that would make you run from the room, or hide under the covers, or make 'just another day' seem impossibly hard.

When digging into why we do what we do, previous negative experience is a big factor. It conditions our behaviour even if we're not aware of it (once bitten, twice shy), sometimes bringing wisdom, other times paranoia. Our motives can't be fully mapped; they have many tendrils. But there will be key experiences – what we might call 'defining moments' which are formative. They might empower us. They may, equally, injure us in ways that leave debilitating scars.

These can be one-off experiences or constants in our lives. We can find these sharp edges in our relationships with others, especially when that relationship is hard-going, even destructive. Some things – some people – shatter us.

Life has sharp edges. And sometimes we bleed.

> *looking to rediscover*
> *wholeness, I examine*
> *myself and try to cover*
> *my bruises, soothing*
> *them with the balm*
> *of distraction.*
> *seeking an escape*
> *from the inescapable –*
> *that I do not know how*
> *to mend my fractures,*
> *to restore serenity.*

> *continually turning*
> *towards you, and then*
> *away from you, fearing*
> *the sting of cure, or*
> *the disappointment*
> *of incurability.*
> *I look to the bruises*
> *and realise I do not*
> *always remember*
> *the blows, the source*
> *of the darkness, only*
> *a hotchpotch collection*
> *of irritants, which*
> *preserve the streaks*
> *as violet.*

The fragile core

When we describe someone as heartbroken, often we mean disappointed in romantic love. Someone has left them; love is unrequited or been withdrawn. We think of those cracked-open heart shapes.

What if we reflect on the heart not as the red-Valentine-card shape, nor even the pump sending blood around the body, but as the true *core* of a person? To be thus broken is not the sole territory of romantic love, but of all loves and human experience. A person's heart – the core of their being – can be shattered by traumatic experiences, by the actions of others, by loss, violence, abuse. It can end up in a state of constant breaking – the shattered pieces never really going back together properly.

How can this core become whole again? We turn to all the things and experiences we think might heal us, including the 'knight in shining armour' ideal. We wait and put our lives on hold, pinning our hopes on something that never arrives. If someone comes into our lives, someone generally good and kind, who needs love just as we do, we can heap them so high with our expectations – that they should 'save' us, heal us – that we end up disappointed. They, in turn, feel devalued because they can never be good enough, strong enough, helpful enough.

We clutch at them and resent sharing them with others. We want them all to ourselves because they are everything to us. Should not we, then, be everything to them? We cling to them until they feel trapped. The expectation wears them down. Our painful jealousy makes us irritable, accusatory. It makes them back away, away from our sharp tongues and reproachful glares. As the distance widens, the jealousy gets worse.

Updating our expectations

Things fall apart, whether this takes place in family relationships, between friends or between lovers, or in our more distant perceptions of public figures. We are disappointed. We build people up to an impossible extent and then tear them to shreds once the inevitable fall occurs. When someone fails us utterly, hurting us beyond belief, that causes another core-breaking, because all our worth was based in that person or that relationship. We find we neglected everything and everyone else. The safety nets are not in place.

We can enter any relationship assuming things will be a certain way because we would like them to be that way, or because it's been held up as 'ideal'. We may come across what appears to be a shining example of such a relationship and be alarmed by all the dullness and scratches in our own. Comparison, as usual, gets us nowhere. We cannot know the backstory to every life and every relationship. We may need to update our expectations and rearrange our worldviews.

What on earth are we trying to find, anyway?

A saviour, a healer, a lover who won't desert us, someone who is aboundingly kind, *always* enough, someone worth the signing over of our souls, casting aside the power of possession and instead allowing ourselves to be owned, in a profound rather than prosaic way, by another?

Someone who would sacrifice everything for us, forgive us again and again, someone who will always be there, someone who is the only one who can ever meet our needs, someone who has been seeking us, whom we have sought even when we didn't know it, someone whose love is never ending, to whom we can give our lives?

> *... by his bruises we are healed.*
> Isaiah 53:5b

REFLECT

- What factors in your life do you think have 'sharp edges'?
- Have you experienced a 'core-breaking'?
- Give yourself some time to reflect and pray about these things.

Sometimes I terrify myself –
this swarm within my heart –
so many beasts that fly within,
the buzzing making it hard to hear you;
so much that can tear my tender faith
with incessant poking and pulling at it
prod, prod, prodding.

I sift the waters of my mind
hoping for the glitter of gold
amid the dust and murk.
God, where are you?

Have I mistaken you for someone else,
or identified something else as you?
Are you there at all, and have I got you right?
Don't leave me, Saviour of my soul.
Do not lose your grip on me.
Everlasting arms, uphold me,
for my safety nets are wearing thin.

Give me an undivided heart,
reassemble the far-flung pieces
and bring me back.
God, bring me back.

Chapter 5

What on earth possessed you?

*'If you want to be perfect, go, sell your possessions
and give to the poor, and you will have treasure in heaven.
Then come, follow me.'*
Matthew 19:21 (NIV)

There are so many Things.

Things to make life better, easier, more bearable, more delightful, more meaningful, more... just *more*. Things that meet our desires, express who we are, or help us avoid what we want to ignore. Things we invest in, work with, collect, explore, buy, play with and throw away. Things to dull some of those sharp edges of life, to patch our wounds and ease our discomfort.

Happiness for sale?

Complete the sentence: 'I wouldn't want to be without my...'

We get attached to objects. They can have an associative value, or be tools for doing something that would otherwise be difficult or impossible. We grow accustomed to them; we've shaped our lives around them.

Objects can bring us pleasure. That is not the same as relying on objects for our deep-down happiness, but sometimes the line between them gets blurred. We move from simple enjoyment to a stronger attachment. Not only do we like things to fulfil their function, we like them to look and feel nice. *We like our things to be beautiful.* Soon we are saying 'I *can't* be without my...'

Most of us, if that 'thing' was taken away from us, would experience frustration, perhaps sadness, if it has sentimental value. We may rely on it for a particular task. The lack of the tool causes inconvenience. If it's what we consider an 'essential', we fret. The last thing we need in a busy week is the freezer breaking down, or a flat tyre on a bank holiday weekend.

What *is* an essential? In the not-so-distant past, mobile phones were luxuries. Now, with sleek and light designs, the capacity to connect, take photos, act as your diary, they may be considered essential, at least to those with certain lifestyles. It's used not just for leisure but for work. It's not a survival necessity (unless needed to make an emergency call), but can be central to a certain way of living – one that is becoming the norm. We use it to work or get in touch with someone or keep abreast of what's going in the world.

Money can make a positive difference to someone's life when used wisely and distributed fairly. 'Money can't buy happiness' in itself, but it can enable us to do things that bring us pleasure – to travel and see new places, to pursue a hobby or go out for a meal, to buy the tools for connecting with friends and family. It can get us food, clothes and housing, which eases worry, because then we're not lacking for our basic needs.

Investment on a wider scale can aid general 'happiness levels' by enhancing overall standards of living. We can decrease child mortality rates, improve maternal health, provide sanitation facilities. Money can do good things if directed well.

Money and morality

However, the lure of 'riches' is an age-old craving, accompanied by equally ancient warnings:

> Do not wear yourself out to get rich;
> be wise enough to desist.
> When your eyes light upon it, it is gone;
> for suddenly it takes wings to itself,
> flying like an eagle toward heaven.
> Proverbs 23:4-5

Money and possessions facilitate aspects of our lives, enabling us to do specific things and live in certain places. They allow us to reach a certain standard of living and can give us a sense of security. Yet they can be stolen, destroyed or unfairly distributed.

'Give me neither poverty nor riches, but give me my daily bread,' says Agur, in Proverbs 30. 'Otherwise I may have too much and disown you and say "who is the Lord?"'(vv.8-9, NIV). To have 'too much' can pull us away from our provider. As Jesus put it, 'you cannot serve both God and wealth' (Matthew 6:24). Wealth can exert a kind of mastery. It can end up marring our lives, not bettering them. Riches claim our loyalties and create a deep divide between those who have and those who have not.

In early 2017, Oxfam published a paper saying that eight men owned the same amount of wealth as the poorest half of the world.[6] The distribution of wealth is by no means equal. Wealth defines not just the rich but the poor, dividing us and keeping us in our places of power or of powerlessness. The amount someone has can affect their position in society and the world. Poverty becomes a prison. It's easy to get into cycles of debt – to survive, we borrow more. If we borrow for what we don't really need, eventually we will have to borrow for what we *do* need, because our resources have been used up paying off the original debt. Loan companies make it sound so simple – an instant solution to your problem – but the long-term result can be misery. The borrowers are no long owners but *owned*.

'The love of money is the root of all evil.' Many forget the first three words of this sentence, but they are essential. The surrounding verses are worth reading:

> *... there is great gain in godliness combined with contentment; for we brought nothing into the world, so that we can take nothing out of it; but if we have food and clothing, we will be content with these. But those who want to be rich fall into temptation and are trapped by many senseless and harmful desires that plunge people into ruin and destruction. For the love of money is a root of all kinds of evil, and in their eagerness to be rich some have wandered away from the faith and pierced themselves with many pains.*

1 Timothy 6:6-10

When we find this craving within us, or a delight in our bank balances, we need to be wary. Because it is in pursuit of money and power that many evils have been ignored or even caused. Money has no morals. It is just another thing, but in our world it symbolises power, control and self-sufficiency. With it we can get *more* things, and be 'trapped by many senseless and harmful desires'.

Chasing money can mean that lines get blurred and ethics get hazy. We end up 'piercing ourselves with many pains' – and others, too. This is a pastoral concern for the church, not just a general warning. We chase money and we cling to it. We are then afraid of losing it. We try to think up ways of getting more of it.

[6] *An economy for the 99%*, Deborah Hardoon (Oxfam International, January 2017). Some criticised the report for 'unfairly' highlighting these eight men, who included at least one major philanthropist, but this missed the point – that *this is how things are*.

The love of money has the power to divide a heart.

We think we want something and then, perhaps, we get it. After the initial thrill, the satisfaction wears off and we find ourselves once more in a state of lack. *I want.* We imagine that when we possess this or have achieved that, we will be happy. We stake our contentment on having these things, dreaming of them, anticipating them and then... anti-climax. It turns out to be not the top of the ladder but just another rung. We want bigger and better and extra and more. A newer model, a sleeker design, more room, more potential for making us happy. If I only I could have... then I would be content.

Some propose that there is a plateau when, after a certain amount of wealth is accrued, happiness levels are no longer affected.[7] Others suggest that we all have our own default level of happiness, to which we revert when other influencers have waned.[8] Whatever the case may be, to assume that 'more' always equals 'happier' is not healthy for us.

Hoarders

At first, all we want is 'enough'. Then perhaps a few little 'luxuries'. But travel too far down the road and love of money becomes its own end. This can be a reaction against previous poverty. For others, hoarding seems to be for hoarding's sake – their lives' purpose is to get more money, to have more things. It's where they find their value. In fact, the quest becomes instinctive – it may not even be something they themselves can explain. They just want more of it.

Hoarding doesn't always mean money grabbing. There are those who struggle to get into their houses because they have crammed them so full of stuff, where even an old, rusty can is kept because it might be useful. The piles of newspapers, carrier bags and other things clogging the hallway become somehow so connected to the owner's sense of control and safety that the idea of getting rid of them feels terrifying.

We can get attached to anything. Sometimes these attachments are part of some deep-down problem or disorder; sometimes they

[7] A Princeton University study (Daniel Kahneman and Angus Deaton, 2010) suggested that, in the USA, incomes rising above $75,000 made no difference to emotional well-being. They concluded that 'high income buys life satisfaction but not happiness' and 'low income is associated both with low life evaluation and low emotional well-being' (www.pnas.org/content/107/38/16489.abstract)
[8] This is known as the set-point theory of happiness.

are the end of a journey that started years ago, but we didn't realise where it was taking us. The primary motivation of our lives becomes not just to accumulate new things but to guard fiercely what we have already accumulated. It has become part of who we are, intrinsic to our identity. *We do not know who we are without it.*

We can be cheated into thinking things are necessities when they are not (many advertisements make the most of this). Psychologically, we *can* become attached to things and get stressed without them. When they are taken from us we feel deprived, or don't know how to cope, even if they are non-essentials.

If we invest ourselves in what we possess, it's hard to let go. The rich young ruler who questioned Jesus 'went away sad' after being told to give up his possessions (Luke 18:23). Perhaps Jesus had seen that the man's attachment to his possessions was too strong, too tied up with his identity. How much of our identity and sense of value do we invest in what we own? If we have that great an attachment to our possessions, we need to think about what that means in terms of what motivates us and where we find meaning in our lives.

Could we give it up, if Jesus asked it of us?

We get attached not just to physical possessions but positions, roles, information. We embed ourselves so firmly into these that we are nervous of exploring who we are without them; we bury ourselves deeper so that we don't have to face the things that bother us deep down, the feelings of insecurity or hurt or emptiness, or just the horrible feeling that we are 'nothing without it'.

We do not want to be nothing.

The right kind of treasure

Every biblical exhortation to be and do (or not do) ties in with the whole package of what it means to live, love and serve. Separating out one issue becomes a puzzling thing – of course it does, because we have removed it from the framework in which it is designed to operate. Good stewardship impacts many areas of our lives.

To possess, to have, to accrue – these drivers can be fraught with anxiety, selfishness and instability. They do indeed lead us to pierce ourselves with unnecessary pains. Better, it seems, to be content as far as we are able, and to live with generous hearts, taking care of one another and making up for the gaps – and here again is the rub, because to do so we all need to show compassion and concern, to be willing to share. To handle money well and wisely, we need to do it together. In a world in which we all protect our individual piggy banks, this can be a challenge.

The letter to Timothy continues:

> As for those who in the present age are rich, command them not to be haughty, or to set their hopes on the uncertainty of riches, but rather on God who richly provides us with everything for our enjoyment. They are to do good, to be rich in good works, generous, and ready to share, thus storing up for themselves the treasure of a good foundation for the future, so that they may take hold of the life that really is life.

1 Timothy 6:17-19

Hoarding is not a biblical principle; we are warned against it. We are to store up less tangible things, not that of material treasures but something with the flavour of eternity. As Jesus said: 'Where your treasure is, there is your heart.' (Matthew 6:21) The rich who hoard at the expense of the poor get short shrift. Instead they are called to be generous with what they have and be 'ready to share'.

In telling the Parable of the Rich Fool, Jesus demonstrates that it is pointless to store up riches for ourselves. We are to be 'rich toward God' instead. 'Be on your guard against all kinds of greed,' Jesus says, 'for one's life does not consist in the abundance of possessions.'[9]

Our lives do not consist in the abundance of possessions. We are not to be defined by these things, nor are we to give them a value that should be reserved for other, much greater, things.

Lift my eyes, O God,
above these trinkets and treasures
I have amassed for myself.
Give me a glimpse of another picture,
of riches of a different kind
of blessing and hope and compassion and grace
of pearls of great price
found only in You.

REFLECT
- What can't you live without?
- Have financial concerns ever made you feel trapped?
- What is a healthy attitude towards our possessions?

[9] Luke 12:13-21

Part II
Boxes and Straitjackets

Chapter 6
The lenses of our lives

For now we see in a mirror, dimly,
but then we will see face to face.
Now I know only in part;
then I will know fully,
even as I have been fully known.
1 Corinthians 13:12

How do you see me? What is it that you are seeing me through?

Your spectacles may or may not be rose-tinted, but they will be tinted with *something*.

That which shapes our lives also shapes our view of the world. We see through our own cultures and value systems. We may be optimistic or pessimistic. We might have a strong belief in something beyond ourselves – or an equally strong belief that there is no such thing. We have our own ideals and ethics – those we've been taught, those we've claimed for ourselves, those we've embraced, rejected or replaced.

What we know about the world colours everything we look at. We won't often be aware of it, as it is unconscious, automatic. We are *wearing* the lenses of our worldviews, not looking *at* them.

We are shaped not just by what we see but how we see it.

Questions of context

'I don't understand where you're coming from' is a familiar phrase. The view from over here is just not the same as it is over there.

We frame things – ideas, experiences, beliefs – within our own understanding of the world. Some things transfer easily across contexts and cultures; other times we end up reshaping them to 'fit' into our way of seeing things. This can result in attaching new meaning to them, whether this is deliberate or accidental. Sometimes we adapt things too much, so that something important is lost or a compromise goes too far. We repaint it in our own colours.

You can't grab something wholesale out of one worldview and apply it directly to another without acknowledging and understanding the original context. There'll be nuances you miss, background information you don't have. It just doesn't mean the same to you, so the whole thing becomes a hotbed of misunderstanding.

Imagine a culture in whose history an heroic, short-haired person stood up against a rather nasty long-haired person. As a testimony to the good person, who overpowered the wicked person to great acclaim, everyone decided to cut their hair. Eventually, to have short hair became associated with being a good person. It was a powerful symbol of something that inspired them, a declaration of intent to lead a good life.

Then someone from that culture travels to another country, where all the people have long hair. This shocks the visitor. Obviously, these people don't care about being good! He then declares: 'You must cut your hair. Don't you know that only bad people have long hair?' Word spreads and so begins a whole new hairdressing cult, which no one really understands. Its followers are mocked for their belief that *having short hair makes you a good person*. The original story – the reason for the tradition – was never passed on.

It's a silly example, but lenses can limit our perceptions, so that we make assumptions and unfair judgements about what other people think and believe. We don't understand why they believe something, nor know where the belief originated. The context to something can be 'lost in translation'. We may need to reinfuse it with meaning and, in doing so, understand and respect it; we may need to identify a different symbol for it; we may need to challenge the assumption behind it.

There will be times when an entire worldview *needs* recolouring; the new lenses are better than the previous ones. This can be a difficult process. You're not just changing the furniture, you're rebuilding the whole house.

Our worldviews, our belief systems, the lenses through which we look at life, the boxes we make for ourselves – these things help define us, tell us who we are or, at least, who we *think* we are.

Be aware of your boxes. They shape you more than you know.

Masquerade

Sometimes our worldviews and belief systems are very structured. Beliefs can be interwoven and reliant on each other – tugging at one thread is perceived as a threat, resulting in a defensive response or a quiet, tortured unravelling. Each belief depends on another.

At other times, conflicting beliefs are held in a fragile alliance. We don't focus on their inconsistencies, but they shape us nonetheless. If we try to hold together such an incoherent worldview, we can be motivated by a need to keep it together. We fear disintegration. Unfortunately, this can mean the whole system can collapse – we end up turning our backs on the entire thing, rather than dealing directly with its incoherencies.

Sometimes we have a 'show' version of our worldview, as we struggle to grasp what we *actually* believe. We portray certainty, but deep down we grapple not just with doubt but *unknowing* – we ourselves cannot tell what we believe. There are so many layers, so many pieces we can't quite make fit.

Sometimes we feel we have to conform to a template. We fret that we'll be 'found out' if we don't. We know the right things to say; we know how to fit in. We can make a 'copy' of a worldview we once had but lost. Or we've existed so long in the company of others that we do a passable imitation of it – sometimes seeming *more* genuine than those who really believe it!

We all have the ability to pretend – to others, to ourselves, to God. Pretence can become a habit. It is possible to make a show of faith. We can know the 'right words'. We might even convince others. But the God we dismiss in secret sees us and is not fooled by our words. 'Not everyone who says to me, "Lord, Lord", will enter the kingdom of heaven…' (Matthew 7:21).

The prospect of unravelling frightens us; we fear to confess our feelings, so we hide behind the script. We don't tackle these feelings, or share them with those who might help us.

We hide from God. Which is foolish, for if there is a God of the sort we claim to profess, he is unbefuddled by our 'hiddenness'. There is no hiding from God. As that famous Psalm declares: 'Where can I go from your spirit? Or where can I flee from your presence?' (Psalm 139:7)

A fissure opens up within us, between the part that professes belief, reciting the words with ease, and the turmoil-ridden, howling part that dare not express itself. Will this schism become wider? Will we become so adept at ignoring it that we stay in the shallows all our lives, never daring to hit the deep, lest the truth will out? Can we cover up a heart so divided? Or will we disintegrate entirely, one day exploding out of the mask, turning our backs on everything and never believing in anything beyond our 'self' – perhaps, not even that?

Beliefs about ourselves

Beliefs are powerful, especially 'core beliefs' – that which we believe deep down about ourselves and the world. They are the lenses of our lives. They both drive us and define us.

Psychotherapy can challenge a 'core belief' that has been identified as damaging or toxic. It may be buried under a load of surface stuff which looks healthy enough, but the root is twisted and painful. Those who believe – at their core – that they are 'worthless' will express this in their lives. They may deny that is what they think. They may not even realise they think it. Unpeeling the layers to get to that core belief is painful.

The boxes we create may be flexible but can also be rigid. Sometimes they are so cleverly built that we don't notice how boxed in we are. We don't even realise that there is a whole world outside our perception of it. When we encounter those who identify themselves differently, we are confused, even threatened. And when they come with their own 'boxes' and see us as equally puzzling, misunderstandings and conflict can arise.

Another way of looking at this is to talk about *mindsets*. These are *sets* of assumptions we hold about ourselves, as individuals or as a group. They affect how we approach life.

In her book, *Mindset*, psychologist Dr Carol Dweck differentiates between *fixed* mindsets and *growth* mindsets.[10] These relate to how we learn and how we perceive our own capabilities. A fixed mindset tends to believe that our abilities and talents are set in stone. We have a certain amount of intelligence and that's not going to change. We're good at what we're good at, we're not good at what we're not good at. Fixed mindsets do a lot of labelling – failure, success, good, bad.

A growth mindset has softer edges. Just because something is hard doesn't mean we can't learn to do it. A growth mindset praises the effort rather than the result. It sees potential for change and, unsurprisingly, *growth*.

For someone with a fixed mindset, a failed attempt can make them dub themselves a failure. They assume they are 'rubbish' at whatever it is they tried to do. They are more inclined to give up.

[10] *Mindset: how you can fulfil your potential*, Dr Carol S. Dweck (Random House, 2006; published in the UK by Robinson, an imprint of Constable & Robinson Ltd., 2012)

(If they *already* believe they are a failure, this just reinforces that belief.)

Those with a growth mindset note the failure but see it as a learning opportunity rather than a statement about who they are. *What can I do differently? What do I learn from this?* They are more inclined to try again.

Reshaping the view

My chains fell off, my heart was free,
I rose, went forth, and followed Thee.
Charles Wesley

The lens of the Christian story is one of transformation. We are urged to 'be transformed by the renewing of [our] minds' (Romans 12:2). Our worldviews are reshaped into a different pattern, as we grasp more of grace, as we follow Jesus more closely. We are called to change and grow. Growth is intrinsic to a Christian life and mentality, because we are disciples. We follow and listen and learn; we are consoled and we are challenged.

Grasping what God says about us, rather than what we, or others, think, can be mind-blowing – but hard, initially, to compute. However, when the core belief is shattered, something radical and transformative takes place. Because it was a core belief, our whole sense of identity shifts. Core beliefs aren't easily broken. But the Holy Spirit has the power to make them crumble.

It can be sudden, based on a spiritual encounter or experience; it may be a slow process until one day the last link in the chain falls open and we are freed of its ugly hold on us.

Our worldview is still limited, we don't have fully functioning lenses yet. There are some things we still don't understand, things we don't have the wisdom or strength to see.

But we are called onwards, our eyes on the one we follow, for that one is the Way, Truth and Life to us, and that much we know.

Open my eyes, Lord.

REFLECT
- What lenses are you wearing – how do they shape your life?
- Have you ever 'played the part' of a worldview?
- Do you believe we have the potential to change?

My world – what colour is it?
As I see through my glass darkly...
I wonder, if the smudges I am seeing
are part of the landscape
or only dust in my eyes.

I know that when I wake,
the view can look different –
what excited me yesterday
I fail to see today, when tiredness
or discouragement
steal my vision.

And on the wider plane of life
what truths or, indeed, lies
direct my sight?
Lord, help me recognise
the things through which
I watch my world.

Chapter 7
Define me!

'Who are you?' said the Caterpillar.
This was not an encouraging opening for a conversation.
Alice replied, rather shyly, 'I-I hardly know, sir, just at present – at
least I know who I was when I got up this morning,
but I think I must have been changed several times since then.'
'What do you mean by that?' said the Caterpillar sternly.
'Explain yourself!'
'I can't explain myself, I'm afraid, sir' said Alice,
'because I'm not myself, you see.'
'I don't see,' said the Caterpillar.
'I'm afraid I can't put it more clearly,' Alice replied very politely, 'for I
can't understand it myself to begin with;
and being so many different sizes in a day is very confusing.'
'It isn't,' said the Caterpillar.
Lewis Carroll
Alice's Adventures in Wonderland

Who are you?

Are you an assortment of genetic material? Is your identity formed by where you've been, what you've seen, heard, learned? Are you a product of your environment, a child of your culture, typical of your age? Yes, yes and, probably, yes.

But 'Who are you?' can be a difficult question to answer, even if we have, unlike Alice, been the same size all day long.

Searching for our identity

'Define me, define me!' mocks psychiatrist Roger in US sitcom *Friends*, analysing girlfriend Phoebe's friendship group. Naturally, he gets the boot. But many of us do crave a sense of definition in our lives.

How *do* we define ourselves? When someone asks, 'who are you?', we respond with our names. If we feel the need to expand on this, we might add where we're from, explain the nature and place of our employment, reference our family or point out mutual friends. These are all shapers of our identity, mini-moulders and motivators, so it's natural for us to look to them to help us answer the question.

But many of us recognise that these can't fully encapsulate who we are. Grounding our sense of identity in them can be tricky. What if we don't have a fixed point we call home, or have never known such a thing, or have lived in so many places we cannot identify with just one? Who are we then?

What if we hate our day jobs, are unemployed, or can't work because of illness or other circumstances? What if it's hard to explain 'what we do'? Who are we then?

What if we're dealing with relationship breakdown or don't have any living relatives? What if we feel friendless? Who are we then?

Do we simply become the negative? I'm not from anywhere, I don't have employment in the sense that you mean, I'm not attached to anyone. All I have is my name – and it doesn't feel like very much.

Who am I then?

The problem of 'Plan B'

When people hold up an ideal of a meaningful life, we wriggle about if we don't fit. If the ideal, for example, is to 'settle down' and get married and have 2.4 children, what about those who aren't married and don't have children? Are they made to feel lacking, as if there is a life box they haven't ticked? Is *that* who we are – the boxes we have ticked?

There are those who ask such things as, 'Has she found someone yet?' As if that is her sole purpose, as if she is lacking. As if singleness means not being 'fulfilled' (Jesus was single; the apostle Paul recommended it!). As one of my (male) friends put on Facebook recently – 'Not looking for an 'other half', I'm already whole.'

I'm already whole.

If we are constantly talking about one template of an ideal lifestyle, we will always talk in the language of substitutes, of 'plan Bs'. As if we've missed out, as if we are second-best. We can spend our entire lives feeling that we missed out, that the primary box on our to-do list *never got ticked*. We either live our lives trying to tick that box, or protesting that we shouldn't *have* to tick it in order to be 'whole'.

What are we saying, if women and men are defined as wivesin-waiting and husbands-to-be, or potential mothers or fathers? What happens if their lives go down a different path?

We need to challenge the stereotypes of what our lives should be. I'm married, but I don't have children. Thankfully, we're rarely quizzed about it, although it does feel awkward when people make their own assumptions as to why. In general, I have peace about our situation. This peace can be jarred when I come up against societal expectations of what my life should be. Expectations implying that I am 'missing out', that I am never quite fulfilled. That's when it chafes. Am I missing out? Well, yes – in that it's an experience I don't have. It is a profound experience, of that I have no doubt. But to imply I am not a whole person...?

Ticking the parenthood box won't make you immune to further expectation. I've realised this when the conversation widens and everyone feels allowed to be honest! Parents of an only child are grilled: 'When are you are having another one?' Women are eyed up for suspected waist-expansion. There are those who struggle profoundly under the weight of expectation as to what 'kind of parents' they should be. If they feel unhappy in their parental role, it's sometimes implied that they are ungrateful, or 'bad' parents. The responsibility of caring for a child is enormous; the reams of advice about the 'right thing to do' can be terrifying. (It terrifies me, and I'm not a parent!)

Accidental isolation
Life takes many forms with many blessings (and the accompanying hardships and challenges). What about those who desperately want children and haven't been able to have them for whatever reason? Expectation only adds an unnecessary layer of awkwardness to the depth of their grief.

Parenthood can feel very isolating. Your children may bring you unique, irreplaceable joy, but this does not mean you feel wonderfully fulfilled at every moment of the day (especially when a screaming toddler writhes on the floor, while you scrape congealed paint out of the cat's whiskers, worrying about the rash on your baby and battling your own tears of exhaustion).

We all cope with these things differently. We all have different strengths and weaknesses. Many of us feel like we 'never get it right'. If we overload marriage (or any romantic relationship) with the unhealthy expectation of meeting all each other's needs, it's a strain. Being in a relationship doesn't mean you can't be hideously lonely at times. Do we admit this, in all our template-toting?

When we divide ourselves by relationship or parental status, we deny each other the value of each other's support and companionship – *whatever our own situation might be.* We also need to acknowledge other people's longings and not dismiss them. I remember being a bit condescending in my late teens / early 20s of friends who were 'looking for a husband'. It irritated me; I wanted them to feel fulfilled without the need for a partner. I felt that, by making this their primary goal, they were devaluing themselves as individual women and putting their lives on hold. I meant well, but who on earth was I to judge their longing to share their lives with someone, or make assumptions about how they were feeling and where those feelings came from? (A lot of damage can be done by those who 'mean well'.) *Their journey was their own.* It was my privilege to share it with them.

I wonder, can we stop judging and envying each other's situations and instead start sharing them together in a sensitive way, recognising our different circumstances – joy, pain and all? Can we be family together in a wider sense, a community of loving diversity?

God has blessed me with many experiences as a married-without-children person. I have found great meaning in my journey as a writer, a journey I could not have managed as a mother (partly because of my health issues). 'That's no substitute for a child,' some of the template-toters might say, but that's not what I mean. *I'm not looking for substitutes.* This is not my 'plan B'. I'm looking for how God wants me to live, here and now, in *these* circumstances. That's where I find my wholeness. I want to know how I can explore God's blessings in my life and share that blessing with others, young and old.

On the job

What about our working lives – do we rank some jobs as more worthwhile than others? Do we not understand how someone can be satisfied with their lives if they are doing something we consider too 'menial'? How do we think people feel when we constantly imply that what they are doing means less? We are called to do whatever we do for the Lord (see Colossians 3:17). This should apply whether we deal in food or numbers or clothing or cleaning products or words or transport or politics.

It's one thing to aspire to something you would love to do – but another to imply that we should aim for a particular job in order to have value in the eyes of others. To imply that someone's worth is bound up with the style of their employment is to denigrate their humanity.[11] For those who can't find work, it's a struggle to keep hold of their sense of worth in a system that often dehumanises them.

We can't all have the job we prefer. Sometimes the job we want and enjoy someone else cannot imagine enjoying. But isn't that just a reflection on our differences?

By putting such an emphasis on 'what people do for a living', we can lead some to despair or unnecessary shame, by our constant need for comparison and quantification. Even the fact that some jobs are low paid and others high paid reflects this tendency. Although you would think, in principle, those who have the hardest work should be paid more, it often doesn't work out that way! Our 'reward' system is rarely fair.

But so often we define people by their relationships or their jobs or their salaries or an assortment of other things.

However, what we think of as the primary definers of human living – whether child or parent or spouse or lover or worker or collector of spoons – they all *miss* something.

Why? Because they are all labels. And labels are, by nature, exclusive.

True to type?
I'm an introvert, but I don't tick all the introvert boxes. Plus, I'm always adapting. Changing circumstances affect my behaviour, my viewpoint. I learn deeper things about myself as I see my reactions (and decide whether I like them or not). I've recently come across the term 'ambivert', supposed to cover those who don't fall easily into either introvert or extravert categories. *It turned out the two categories were not enough.*

When boxes become unworkable, we work instead by 'scales' – where are you on a scale of 1 to 10? I hover over it with my pen and think *I have no idea.* No wonder so many people circle (5). Somewhere in the middle will do.

Personality types are fascinating. Examining them can bring a sense of freedom and illumination – and help us take steps to learn and grow. But have we got a bit too obsessed with categories?

Whenever I take any kind of personality type test, often my 'answer' doesn't exist on the multiple choice, or two answers seem equally relevant. 'Choose the answer that you are immediately

[11] Of course there are workers whose humanity is denigrated by what they are told to do, but that isn't what I'm talking about here.

drawn to,' I've been told, to trust that initial instinct rather than think too much. But what if that initial instinct varies depending on time of day, mood, age, what happened last week? And besides, if I like to ponder things before I answer, isn't that 'true to type'?

It can be a useful tool. Some of these official tests are designed to free you up to be who you are, to help you understand yourself and how you work with others. But it's not a prison, a seal, a permanent brand burned into our skin for all time. When we think of it like this, it begins to sound like a 'fixed mindset', or at least, plays into it nicely. We don't believe we can be any different and therefore never try to be. The 'type' becomes our badge.

Categorising complexity

Are these techniques helping us or hindering us? I suspect they can do both, depending on how we approach them. A fixed mindset might see them as a permanent result – *this is who I am therefore I am good at that but bad at that and always will be.* A growth mindset might see them as a springboard, an interesting insight into where we are now, but also noting what we would like to see change – how we can work on our weaknesses and use our strengths to their fullest.

It also relies on us telling the truth about ourselves. We could, potentially, fiddle around until we get our desired type, choosing an option *because that is what we want to be* or *because it will result in a certain outcome.* Suddenly we're trying to work out what the next quiz answer is, so we can fit our chosen category.

'It only took me four tries to get Captain Kirk!' Leonard Hofstadter proclaims in an episode of cult TV series *The Big Bang Theory*, as he describes what a good day he's having. These quizzes of 'what character are you?' can indeed be fun (and are different from true personality testing), but even in these minor ways we still want a certain result. We are disappointed when we don't get it. Or someone says, 'I got Captain Kirk, too!'

Oh.

Suddenly you don't feel so special anymore. You realise there's no insight here, that it's not really to do with you at all.

So many boxes;
so many colours.
So many straitjackets
squeezing me tight.
I don't know how
to make myself fit.

Maybe I am in a state of perpetual confusion. Maybe I resent having to make a definitive mark on 'me'. Maybe I am... human. And that, as I stated at the beginning of this book, is precisely what I am.

We talk about being 'only human' and yet our humanity, for all its flaws and vulnerabilities, is not easy to explain. 'Only human' is a relative term, comparing us to something more than human (whether this is the divine or simply a higher ideal of what we aspire to be). As a stand-alone statement, it doesn't work so well. We *are* human.

We try to categorise life in order to understand it, but it is too complex to be categorised! Humanity is not just a set of people who each exist in their own group or 'slot'. One person is not just the sum of their labels. No wonder we struggle to answer the question 'who am I?' We try to come up with an overarching description or list of attributes, but they'll never pin down the full reality.

Who am I, God?
What is it you have made me to be?

REFLECT
- How do you identify yourself?
- Has anyone ever made you feel lacking because of a 'box' you haven't ticked?
- What do you think is a Christian response to this?

Lord, sometimes I feel swamped
by the expectations of others.
I don't fit into their ready-made boxes.
I feel misunderstood.
But you know me – you understand me.
Wherever I go, you are there with me.
You give me worth and identity and purpose.
Help me not to forget that, and give me courage
when the world does not understand.

Chapter 8
The age of the like button

Looking-glass, looking-glass, on the wall,
Who in this land is fairest of all?
The Wicked Queen
in *Little Snow White*, by the Brothers Grimm

Who do you want to be? Who do you want the world to see?

We often project an image to the world. We hide certain parts of ourselves and promote others; we adapt our ways of communicating to get what we want or give a certain impression. We do it in job interviews, on first dates, when we meet someone new.

It's not necessarily a false projection, but it's selective. Would you want that person to know that you had a tantrum when you spilt the coffee this morning? Would you want them to know that yesterday you cried yourself to sleep? Would you want them to know that nasty thing you said to your loved one last week?

Probably not.

We display what we want the world to see, or what we think the *world* wants to see. We have more control over this than we used to, because we live in an image-driven society.

Beautify me

It's now normal – and easy – to take pictures of yourself. Smartphones have 'selfie settings', which reverse the camera so that you can see yourself as you take the picture.

I take occasional selfies. They can be fun ways of sharing and connecting with friends, giving tasters of a moment, recording a feeling or an experience.

Within this culture of selfie-taking, a natural tendency emerges – wanting to look your best for the camera. And these days, photo-editing is no longer the realm of the professionals.

I have wonky front teeth. This can make me self-conscious in a world which idealises the perfect smile. I have loathed their crookedness, then felt guilty for being so vain. In a group picture, the first thing I see is *my teeth*. I confess, on occasion, I have been tempted to photoshop my smile so it's a bit less wonky in pictures of special occasions (yes, it embarrasses me to write that).[12]

Recently I downloaded FaceApp onto my Smartphone, which some friends were sharing on social media for a laugh. This application transforms a photograph of you into 'young' and 'old' versions of yourself; it suggests what you might look like as male – or female. It can also make you smile in the photograph. (A designer for *Empire* magazine went to an art gallery and applied the FaceApp smile setting to gloomy-looking old portraits, with entertaining results.) I tried out the smiley version on a photo of me, out of curiosity. I observed myself with straight teeth. Honestly, it looked weird. I preferred my own teeth!

This app seems to cater for users' amusement rather than vanity.[13] However, there are other apps which are far more focused on making you look perfect. They give you digital makeovers, make you thinner, more 'acceptable' in the eyes of your peers. You can shrink your nose, make your eyes look bigger, plump out your lips and get rid of that annoying mole.

Cultural expectation to 'be beautiful' drives the making of these apps. The selfie age did not *cause* our obsession with self-image. It's been there for some time – in advertising, in magazines with impossibly perfect, photoshopped models. It was there when the first mirror was created and we began to primp and preen; it was there when we caught sight of our reflection in waters below, as did the mythological Narcissus, transfixed by his own beauty. It was there when we began comparing one person against one another, discovering we had a preference as to whom we found 'attractive'.

We find ways of expressing this in newer forms of media. The technology becomes a tool for our tendencies. Some won't have such strong tendencies, but for others, this environment enables them to flourish. New media can become a mechanism for putting across a certain version of ourselves, for meeting the expectation of others. This version is compelling; we can gaze upon these constructions of ourselves as if they were beautiful reflections. We opt for an 'ideal self', how we *wished* we looked; we choose the image we present to the friends and followers we have on social media sites, websites or blogs. We can ensure we have got rid of our blemishes, special settings on our devices aiding our efforts to 'beautify' ourselves.

---

[12] Some people tell me I have a lovely smile, which shows it's all a matter of perspective.

[13] These comments may be out of date by the time this book is published!

True faces

It might be a huge relief to the teen suffering from acne to be able to do a bit of airbrushing. But what happens when their offline self looks so different, despite the concealer dabbed on? A photographic filter or airbrush app doesn't help when you walk into a classroom and all eyes are on you. However, you can see how tempting it would be to create this other, unblemished version to 'put out there', especially when you feel so self-conscious and when your contemporaries can be so cruel, one casual comment destroying an essential part of your self-esteem.

The social media hashtag #nofilter is popular because it is assumed you were using a filter on your photo app to primp up that sunrise or brighten your Saturday night smile.[14] We doubt the authenticity of what we see, because we know how easy it is to change it.

I use new technology quite happily and enjoy taking pictures (including selfies), but like everyone else I would share the one I was most happy with, the one that puts me in the 'best light'. If I'm feeling shabby and bedraggled, I'm less likely to post a photo of myself! It's useful in a digital age to be able to take numerous pictures and select the best 'few' – rather than be immortalised by that red-eyed, somewhat spotty portrait from 1994.

However, this is a sharp curve of change in human history. Younger generations are now living out their critical identity-forming stages online. They are drawn to it as they create their 'ideal self', but the danger comes when this 'self' created by them online becomes their primary understanding of who they are. The airbrushed selfie and confident persona conceal a more tender, hidden self, which struggles to make the very act of *becoming*. If the natural 'flaws' we all possess are covered up, how do young people mature through the challenges of confronting or accepting them?[15]

As with much of the digital age, because it's so new, we cannot yet know what long-term impact these things have –

[14] For the confused: hashtags are words or phrases used on social media, preceded by #. They act as a kind of label so that users can identify other comments and updates on that topic. They have no spaces or punctuation marks. #hashtagdefinition

[15] Cyberpsychologist Dr Mary Aiken discusses teenagers, 'self' and new technology in chapter 5 of *The Cyber Effect* (John Murray, 2016). Among other things, she talks about the 'curation' of selfies, describing the cyber-self as a 'filtered' self that young people, in particular, try to perfect.

negative or positive. Because older generations are learning at the same time as younger generations, the former can't offer so much experience-acquired wisdom. In fact, at a functional level, younger generations are teaching the old. But what about deeper levels of wisdom? We're still trying to work out the best ways to navigate this new environment. How does this affect things like identity and motivation and overall meaning in our lives, especially for younger, still-developing brains?

The power of connection underpins so much – beyond the bright screen, the button click, the impact of the visual. These all add to the appeal of new media, but there is something in the human psyche, something needing both connection and affirmation and approval, which weaves into it. Beyond both hardware and software, there is a humanity trying to understand itself, to build an identity, to live.

Like me, please

Lying on the ground, [Narcissus] gazes on his eyes like two stars ... and his blushing complexion mingled with the whiteness of snow; and everything he admires, for which he himself is worthy to be admired. In his ignorance, he covets himself; and he that approves, is himself the thing approved...

from Ovid's *The Metamorphoses*, Fable VII

We are driven by how we want to appear. It's the age-old desire for approval, with extra bells and whistles (or buttons and screens). We want to be likable and liked – something far more quantifiable in the age of the 'like' button.

We don't want to be dismissed or mocked, we want praise. We want to be told we are beautiful, that we are worth something, that we are going somewhere. Life becomes a quest for 'likes'. Immediate approval and praise are compelling and a good distraction from the feelings of lack we hide in our hearts. Approval has always been an aspect of motivation – now it comes with clicks. Each click makes you feel good and lack of clicks makes you feel bad.

We live in an age of instant feedback. We can enter a cycle where, just as with other desires, what we have is no longer enough. We want *more* approval, *more* popularity. This quest becomes compulsive, a stimulus with an addictive edge.

Some use new media for attention seeking (positive or negative). They will happily incur great disapproval as long as their voices are heard by as many people as possible and attention is heaped upon them. Many internet 'trolls' love to get a reaction out of people, to which they can in turn react. This can result in shouting matches – as undignified online as they are offline.[16]

Behind the tools

I used to say that technology was a tool – it all depended on how you used it. I've since realised that is too simplistic. There are not merely users, but makers. We need to ask: what are they creating, and why? What drives the design of the tools? They are often constructed to be user-friendly, but makers have motives too. Plus, a designer may not be the owner of a brand but an employee of a company. There are many people involved. And with people come motives, bags of them.

Money, of course, is a huge influencer. Some people create apps just because they 'want to get rich'. If there is a money-making motivator, we run into the same problems that often come from 'pursuing riches'. Advertising has a lot of influence – not just in terms of the content (from the user's perspective) but the revenue that comes from it (from the maker's perspective). Even if only to fund their tool, makers often use advertising, especially if they want their apps to be free to use.

To encourage more clicks on advertisements – and therefore more income – the tool is adapted so that you use it more frequently. The result? Something 'hard to put down' – something that compels you to use it every day, every hour even, otherwise you might 'lose out'.[17]

Even if their motives are good – or at least, not *bad* – makers cannot always predict how their tools will or can be used. This can result in 'casualties' of a sort, as more negative uses or side effects are discovered along the way. It can also result in unplanned positives, but in celebrating those we mustn't forget to exercise caution and self-awareness about how we use things. A hammer is useful for knocking in a nail; we would (hopefully) not swing it at someone's head, but if we did, it could do irreversible harm or even kill them. We don't ban hammers, but we recognise their destructive potential.

[16] An internet 'troll' is someone who posts inflammatory and abusive remarks online with the primary motive of upsetting people and provoking them into an emotional response.
[17] Isn't the same true of books? Yes, a book can be designed to be 'unputdownable', but the agenda for selling lots of books is slightly different from something needing continual 'clicks' for revenue.

Neither demonising nor idolising technology will help. Recognising its potential for both good and bad can help inform our choices in how we use the many resources available to us. We need to form 'wells of wisdom' to help us reflect with care on how to proceed, not knee-jerk reacting, not all-embracing, but working to create a network of positive influencers.[18]

If wise people choose not to engage with technology, what does this mean for our increasingly technological society? In whose hands do we want to place our future?

Branding ourselves

In our current climate, you hear a lot of talk about 'building your brand' – something you are known for, your 'niche' in a sea of voices and wannabes. Social media becomes a place to get heard, to create a following, to have more *influence*. For some bloggers and social media users, this becomes an end in itself but, increasingly, certain professions require it as well.

As a writer today, I'm told I need to 'sell' myself. Publishers value an author's 'platform' – their visibility, their networks, anywhere they can be seen and heard. It's about publicity. However, when what you're doing is something as personal as writing, the line between promoting self and promoting the work is a tricky one and often blurry.

It used to be about finding your voice; now it's about identifying your brand. This feels more prosaic, a bit soul-destroying, less to do with meaning and more to do with appearance (whether that is a correct assumption or not). When something becomes a brand it loses something – depth? Complexity? It becomes *another box*.

This can be particularly problematic for Christian writers and speakers. A platform can be a great way to get the good news out, to act as an advocate for the vulnerable, to demonstrate Christ to the world. But it's a tricky balance when we don't want to seek glory for ourselves. How do we publicise our work (which helps pay the bills) without becoming beacons of branding, puffed-up pedestals of people? One response might be to support and promote each other, but I worry about doing this *quid pro quo* (I don't want to recommend something I think is of poor quality or with which I disagree, just because someone helped to publicise *my* work).

And as we work to 'brand ourselves', we can be tempted to

[18] I realise this is a bit of sweeping statement, rather than a detailed 'how-to', but understanding the motives of both tool-makers and tool-users may provide a good framework for practical 'wisdom' to begin.

do the same as we do when selfie-sharing – we doctor our images, making ourselves into something we're not, or over-emphasising the things that we are, losing a bit of that glorious complexity. We can even make a brand out of honesty and vulnerability, using both our strengths and our weaknesses to draw attention to ourselves.

What 'self' are we sharing? Why?

For wannabe writers or speakers without the name that sells, it can be a disheartening business, but it's a struggle for publishing houses too. Publishers have to ask themselves 'will this sell?', to ensure they themselves keep afloat. It can be a risk to them if they choose to publish solely on the quality of the work rather than the visibility – or existing fame – of the author. Yes, the work may speak for itself, but people need to read it in order to 'hear' it and recommend it to others. As one publisher told me in a pleasantly toned but somewhat exasperating rejection email: 'You have something important to say, but will people perceive they need to hear it?' In other words, *will people buy it?*

Anyone self-employed will need to promote their work in an increasingly competitive world. And what about those seeking employment under someone else? The same often applies – sell yourself in the interview, sell yourself on your CV, sell your product, sell your ideas – not just in the literal sense of selling for money but for success, for reputation, for acceptance in the field.

You'd be forgiven if you started feeling like a *commodity.*

Does this leak into our personal lives? Do we constantly need to promote a certain aspect of ourselves, have a spiel we use to describe ourselves, as we're not sure what or who else to be?

By branding ourselves, we give ourselves an assortment of labels, searchable terms and our own unique #hashtags. What do these labels say about us? Do we want to be labelled in this way?

> *Lord, give me a healthy sense of who I am.*
> *Help me stop trying to be something I'm not.*
> *Where I'm tempted to airbrush my image*
> *and glorify myself, bring me back*
> *to your love alone.*

REFLECT
- What image do you try to project to those around you?
- What do you think are the strengths and weaknesses of social media?
- Do you ever feel the need to 'sell yourself'?

[Mortals] look on the outward appearance,
but the Lord looks on the heart.
1 Samuel 16:7

Chapter 9
The stickiness of labels

O! be some other name:
What's in a name? that which we call a rose
By any other name would smell as sweet...
William Shakespeare
Romeo and Juliet

My husband bought a label maker. In case there was any doubt about what it was, he stuck a label on the back of it. It says: 'label maker'.

The labels now on the plugs behind our television unit tell us what is attached to what, which is useful. Labels help when we're following instructions. Without them, we hold up that weird-looking piece and think, 'what is *that*?'.

The way of words
All words are identifiers, ways of expressing things. We stumble sometimes to find the 'right words'. Is this because we need a broader vocabulary? Or because one word lacks the capacity to hold that much meaning, that much subtlety, or that much clarity?

Words collect baggage and can shift in meaning. A word we once used to identify ourselves gets appropriated by something quite alien to what we originally meant by it. A word with beautiful beginnings becomes a cudgel, a judgement, or a sarcastic retort.

Words can have connotations beyond their basic meaning. 'Be some other name,' begged Juliet of Romeo. 'Wherefore art thou Romeo?' She's not asking for his location; *wherefore* means 'why.'[19] '*Why* are you Romeo?' Juliet agonises from the famous balcony. Can't you be someone else, with a different name, without all the associations that come with it, without the division between our two families?

We don't just use labels for objects – the plug for the DVD

[19] The pedant in me feels the need to be condescending and point this out. Sorry. I permit you to roll your eyes.

player is one thing – we use labels for ourselves. Inevitably, there will be those who fall between the cracks, those who don't conform to our labels. We try calling them misfits, or we add a new label. Or we add an extra category to the original. We define and we define... Always, there are the undefined, the unremarked, those who fall between the boxes, who get lost between our labels. We attempt to make our labels more and more inclusive – but eventually make a nonsense of them. Why? Again, because *all labels are exclusive.*

They identify something not just by what it is, but by what it is *not*. A label always misses somebody; it's the nature of a label. There will be some nuance it doesn't pick up, some factor it can't convey, some element that won't squeeze into the original box.

Despite their usefulness, I've always had an inkling that something about labels is divisive. Loose labels can aid our understanding, but if they become straitjackets, they can be uncomfortable, discriminatory, even cruel.

The clamour of the age

In an era of global communication, labels quickly gain ground. In a different era, they might have been contained to one region, or grown more slowly in meaning. Now, analysis takes place immediately; we don't bother waiting for historical hindsight; we excitably dub This Age and That Age and then get a little anxious when life refuses to be classified. 'What is this we are seeing?', we ask, poking at a passing thought as if it were a whole philosophy. Maybe it is, maybe it will be, or maybe on the grand stage of history it will just become part of the general clamour.

Echo chambers, fake news, gossip-gone-global, shrill voices and shriller counterparts. We try to identify all the components but stepping back, it's a whole lot of noise and hard to understand when you're mixed up in it.

We fling labels on social media, create buzzwords and phrases and then declare them old-hat and out of date a year later. So 2016 was the year of [insert your favoured phrase here], we claim, and pile it up with labels. Imagine a town where people are running around clutching their label makers, sticking labels everywhere and on everyone. Is that picture really so unreal?

There are those who resist, those who observe all this with quiet perplexity. Maybe these are the majority, but the minority can be so shrill and keen to label, label, label, that it then becomes the dominant voice. Things start to shift, until the weight between majority and minority begins to change. Those in the middle begin to move a different way. The outcome of a vote surprises us. The situation changes, because the middle has moved, and we didn't see it happen.

It's an era of sociological and political turbulence, and it's *chock-full* of labels. It's as if in realising the old labels don't work we have decided to create a dazzling array of new ones, ways to remind us who we are because, frankly, we don't know anymore.

The limitation of labels

Boxes are always lacking – however much bigger on the inside we try to make them, like the TARDIS in *Doctor Who* (or, as one character put it, 'smaller on the outside'). There is no one size fits all. However roomy we think our self-made labels have become, the majority are 'smaller on the outside'. The TARDIS, flying from one piece of sky to the next, is a very, very big box. But it is still a box.[20]

In categorising something, we confine it. Think of the word 'heaven'. How much is contained within that word? Does the meaning hitched to it really reflect it? Words and labels begin to have such a strong association with a certain interpretation or point of view that we see them *without seeing them*. You hear the word, you imagine a fluffy cloud. Or a blue box. But does this reflect their deep-down identity?

We can put people in boxes based on their choices. We reinforce these boxes every time we list our categories, pushing everyone into their relevant pigeonholes.

Some try to wriggle out of them. Eventually they find themselves under a different banner. They may still grieve for what they left behind – the original meaning of the label. This meaning may have been lost, or requisitioned in such an extreme form that they hardly recognise it anymore.

They were once so proud of that label. It was a huge part of their lives; it's painful trying to peel it off. There is a sense of grief when the label has been ditched along with all that it stood for... so much is associated with it.

Labels can attract other labels – subheadings, if you like. You may embrace one, then find other stuff dangling from it, not all of which feels right. You may feel a label has been unfairly hijacked and made into something it was never meant to be. You may feel

[20] For *Doctor Who* fans – it was suggested in a 2013 episode (*Journey to the Centre of the TARDIS*) that the inside of the TARDIS is, in fact, infinite. But I'm using it as an analogy, so forgive me for any inaccuracy. It should also be noted that the Doctor still chooses to go outside the box an awful lot!

appalled by the actions of someone else also laying claim to that descriptor. Then you have to decide whether to defend the label against the action, or lose the label because the action has polluted it, taken it so far that you can't get it back.

Losing a label can be destabilising and distressing, or liberating and life-giving – or a heady mixture of all of them, depending on the level of emotional investment and the memories attached to it. If it's an identifier your family holds dear or one everyone around you wears with pride, to ditch that label can make it look as if you're ditching everything they hold of value (which may not be the case at all, but such is the power of labels). Perhaps you always loathed the label, but find it too sticky to take off. You continually scratch at it.

Our love of labels can take us into some difficult places.

> I loved you once.
> You meant so much –
> I was glad to use you
> as my identifier,
> but now I'm not so sure.
> You don't mean
> the same things anymore.
> Do I peel you off completely?
> How can I keep what is good
> and shrug off what is bad?

A driving force

Labels and categories can do good things. To go back to the introvert/extravert scenario, it's been a relief for some to realise that it's okay to be who we are, that we recharge differently, that we have different strengths. But once an issue becomes popular the pendulum, having swung away from one extreme (e.g. a negative view of introversion), then moves towards the other. We feel compelled to jump on board, to choose which category applies to us and proudly defend it.

When something happens and we react in a way that doesn't match our 'type', we feel untrue to the label. It doesn't fit us. Yet labels can begin to drive and reinforce our behaviour. We attempt to conform to them *just because they're our labels*. They are no longer tools but masters, no longer descriptors but dictators.

Labels provide both explanation *and* motivation. They stick to us and we can feel stuck with them. Originally, we were trying to identify something about ourselves. But labels have power. We can feel we have to stay inside the box, otherwise we are *outside* the box. There we fall into the cracks; we don't fit. You may have identified yourself as a certain 'type'. But what about the thing on the list that doesn't fit you? Do you feel the need to ascribe to it in order to still fit that category?

Labels can become idols. We make them the primary way we identify ourselves. We cluster together with those wearing the same badges. When these badges are threatened or under attack, we fight, because we have pinned our lives, our entire sense of self, on those markers.

Labels can become prisons. We can never behave differently now, we will always be 'marked', we can never break out. We will always be known by it, however untrue it feels. We can cling to the label even if we hate it; we don't know how to do without it.

Perhaps we have branded ourselves as 'failure'; it's almost a point of principle that we live up to that self-judgement. The label becomes a stubborn thing; we claim to detest it, but somehow we'd lose face if we changed it. If someone dares to challenge us – suggesting we might be 'lovable', for example, we can strike back – *no, no I'm not*. The label *unlovable* has become a core belief. Believing beyond this classification seems impossible. Our minds are set on believing it, in spite of new evidence emerging.

Sometimes labels can be ill-fitting and yet somehow expected of us. They become a bar we have to reach, an ideal, something we are told we must be. When we fall short, we are all too aware of the disappointment of those who applied that label. We were meant to be so much more, in their eyes. We weary of their expectations, we cannot reach them. We are inclined to ditch it all and give up.

Negative labels are painful when applied and harder to shrug off. We use them to berate ourselves or to lash out at others. We can brandish them with real malice or wave them in simple thoughtlessness – one can hurt just as much as the other. There is a cartoon depicting someone who, surrounded with praise all day, is haunted by one negative comment. He received many compliments, but they faded throughout the day. When night came, only the painful remark remained, keeping him from sleeping.[21]

---

[21] The cartoon is called 'Jerk' and can be viewed at www.deathbulge.com/comics/155

Life in fragments

When we label ourselves – as members of a wider community, but also within our own lives – we can become an assortment of adjectives, of different parts. We long for wholeness, but life is in fragments. It is divided into compartments, but how do these boxes relate to each other? We try to add meaning and somehow end up losing it.

When everything consists of pieces, we struggle to find a thread between them. Conflicting beliefs end up existing side by side. If we keep them boxed, we may never notice, or at least never admit to such a thing. But one day when the essence of 'us' decides to burst out of the boxes, or simply bleed beyond the pigeonhole in which we've been placed, the problems emerge.

We can't consign ourselves to various labels. We are more, we need more, we are made to be more – to seek something greater, something bigger than all the boxes we make for ourselves.

Definer of my heart,
help me see beyond labels.

REFLECT
- When are labels helpful?
- How many labels have been stuck to you? Were they welcome, or not?
- How do labels affect our future actions?

Happy are those who keep his decrees,
who seek him with their whole heart,
who also do no wrong, but walk in his ways.
Psalm 119: 2-3

Chapter 10
Soul division

Hear, O Israel: The Lord is our God, the Lord alone.
You shall love the Lord your God with all your heart,
and with all your soul, and with all your might.
Deuteronomy 6:4-5

It can be a worthwhile journey to explore our desires, drivers and shapers. By doing so, we develop self-awareness and understanding, identifying causes rather than grappling only with frustrating symptoms.

But how difficult it is to create a precise map of what shapes us, of what makes us who we are!

Categorising things can help us to organise our thoughts. Even to 'create a brand' at a basic level is about letting people know who you are and what it is you represent – both in terms of identifying your role (what it is you do) but also quality or reliability (whether you do it well).

The sum of our parts
What about at an individual level, looking at what makes up a human being? We know our body parts by their labels – arm, leg, nose, toe. We need to be able to identify things. But if we apply this tactic to the more abstract and complex elements of ourselves and what we believe, we divide elements meant to exist as a whole, held in balance or even in tension, but together, nonetheless.

Self, soul, spirit, mind – what a confusing muddle of words we use to describe ourselves! Where does one end and another begin? Are they different or the same? We use classifications to help explain what it means to be human – to identify all that is different within us. But over-reliance on them can result in a kind of fragmentation.

The Israelites were told to love God with heart and soul and strength. The command to love God was a oneness, a thoroughness, demanding every last bit of them.

Traditionally, it was the *heart* that was seen as the centre of a person, involving not only sentiment but intent, plans and thoughts. We now know that the brain is the hub of both thought and feeling. Different parts of the brain have distinct functions, but together they form a working whole.

We often separate what we call the 'heart' and the 'mind', as if one were the centre of emotion and the other of intelligence, one experiential in nature and the other intellectual. We can drive a wedge between them – as if thinking and feeling can't work together. We try to divide learning and experience, thought and feeling, mental exploration and emotional encounter. However, one without the other suffers. If we rely only on feelings, neglecting to reflect and to think, our intellects get rusty. If we ignore feelings, we miss out on transformative experiences (which can also lead us to think differently).

Directing the core

Without the heart's pumping blood the brain would not survive, and 'heart' remains a central metaphor for us today. We often use it to describe the core of our being. This is how we use the word when talking about love or loyalty. An undivided heart, a *united heart*, speaks of a focus in which the various threads of our lives are woven together with one primary purpose, one loyalty, one God.

What makes a heart divide? Any number of things. Diverse desires, conflicting motives, property or money, unadmitted idols, powerful masters or an assortment of minor distractions. Doubt, depression, despair. Lack of focus and forgetfulness or, conversely, memories that hamper us and hinder us. Worries about this, that and the other. Differing interpretations of what we consider 'truth'. Expectations from others and expectations *of* others. Eyes looking in the wrong direction, or all directions at once. Unwillingness to make a leap, or a leap too often leapt.

The list goes on: sin, darkness, evil – whether from outside or in. Temptation. Spiritual battle or spiritual torpor. An obsession with the unimportant.

Those who oppose us, those who befriend us. Those who lead us – intentionally or not. The teaching we give and are given. The mistakes we have made and the mistakes others make, too. We all have different stumbling blocks.

What causes the threads to divide and move, resulting in a knotty tangle instead of a woven whole?

The shifting sea

If any of you is lacking in wisdom, ask God, who gives to all generously and ungrudgingly, and it will be given you. But ask in faith, never doubting, for the one who doubts is like a wave of the sea, driven and tossed by the wind; for the doubter, being double-minded and unstable in every way, must not expect to receive anything from the Lord.

James 1:5-8

There are passages in the Bible that can confuse us, even worry us. For those who struggle with doubt, these verses in James 1 can cause anxiety. However, perhaps we should look a little closer. Who *is* the doubter James is talking about? What characterises this kind of doubt? How might this relate to having a divided heart?

The doubter in James 1 shifts about, as does the sea in its myriad of movements, reacting with wind and tide at any given moment. The picture is one of constant changeability, of loyalties which never settle. There is a deep instability here, a confusion as to life's meaning and purpose. The state has been dubbed 'spiritual schizophrenia' by one commentator,[22] and this seems an apt description. Another describes it as the heart being 'split in its allegiance', never trusting God to give the wisdom that is so generously offered.[23]

You could see it as a kind of hypocrisy, whereby the masks we wear are not our true faces; the words we say are not our true thoughts; the things we claim to want are not our true desires. We dip our toes into faith and then pull them out again, we swim towards the deep end and then back, to-ing and fro-ing so much that there is no way we can receive anything from the God we are thinking about following (but never quite doing so).

We never place ourselves in a position to receive; we are too busy juggling our own motives and allegiances; we can never quite decide what it is we want. We confine faith to a compartment, without applying it to other parts of our lives. In doing so we limit our ability to experience the abundant life and the glorious wisdom that is offered to the children of God.

[22] Douglas Moo, *The Letter of James*, Pillar New Testament Commentary (Eerdmans, 2000) p.63
[23] Scot McKnight, *The Letter of James*, New International Commentary on the Old Testament (Eerdmans, 2011) p.92

Friendship and enmity

These verses are about *character* – of a generous God, who gives 'ungrudgingly'. This contrasts with the description of the doubter, who is plagued by inconsistency and divided allegiances.

The doubter is double-minded. The Greek word translates literally as *double-souled*. James has a deep interest in wisdom, fairness, and faith expressed in action. He also talks about prayer. In 1:5-8 he tells those who lack wisdom to *ask God* – a God who gives generously (the Greek can also mean sincerely and/or single-minded). God is willing to give us wisdom, in sincere generous purpose. The double-minded person in many ways is an opposite of this. Her purpose is not sincere nor single-minded but torn in two. *Double-souled*, as if two entities are at war. Is this James's way of describing a divided heart?

The word is only found one other time in the Bible – later in James, when the writer extols his readers:

> Draw near to God, and he will draw near to you.
> Cleanse your hands, you sinners, and purify your hearts,
> you double-minded.
>
> James 4:8

Who does James have in mind here? We read earlier in this chapter:

> Those conflicts and disputes among you, where do they come from? Do they not come from your cravings that are at war within you? You want something and do not have it; so you commit murder. And you covet something and cannot obtain it; so you engage in disputes and conflicts. You do not have, because you do not ask. You ask and do not receive, because you ask wrongly, in order to spend what you get on your pleasures. Adulterers! Do you not know that friendship with the world is enmity with God? (4:1-4a)

Perhaps here we come close to what a divided heart might look like – requesting one thing but secretly wanting another, asking for its own pleasure under the pretence of concern for others. Desire gone bad can create in us a double-souledness, an inconsistency in our lives. To those who are in this state, James cries, 'purify your hearts'! Come back, draw near. God in turn will draw near to you.

The people to whom James is writing to are asking for the wrong things, pursuing selfish motives, at war with their own desires. No wonder they are tossed like waves in the wind. Their focus is not on a trustworthy God, but on themselves.

'Adulterers!' James accuses. A strong word, reeking of unfaithfulness. You can't be friends with God *and* the things of the world.

Back in the Old Testament, Elijah asked the Israelites, 'How long will you go limping with two different opinions? If the Lord is God, follow him, but if Baal, follow him.' (1 Kings 18:21) The NIV translates this as 'how long will you waver', but the NRSV's 'limping' appeals to me as a picture. The doubter James talks about shifts like the sea in the wind; Elijah perceives that the Israelites are hampered, even wounded, by their divided loyalties. By trying to follow two masters, by never giving full allegiance to one alone, followers injure themselves and their walk with God.

They are trying to look two ways at once. Hence, they never see clearly, walk unhindered, or receive the full extent of what is being offered to them.

A divided heart deceives others and deceives self. A divided heart says one thing and means another. A divided heart has a duplicity within it, whether intentional or not. A divided heart tries to split itself between two masters. These might be external, but can also be a matter of self versus God, of flesh versus Spirit.

These are not compatible.

However, all is not lost. Just as Elijah called on the Israelites to make up their minds, James wrote his letter to persuade his readers to be different. *Don't be like this,* he says. *Don't be double minded.*

Unite your hearts.

Inconsistent living

... with flattering lips and a double heart they speak.

Psalm 12:2

James also challenges inconsistency in speech: 'With [the tongue] we bless the Lord and Father, and with it we curse those who are made in the likeness of God' (3:9). Those who consider themselves 'religious' and yet don't 'bridle their tongues' deceive themselves, James says; 'their religion is worthless' (1:29). This is a challenge today, as we all clamour to communicate our opinions. Do we remember to keep a tight rein on our tongues when using social media or email, as well as in our offline interactions? Do we do the equivalent of cursing each other while claiming to praise God? What does this mean for our excessive 'labelling'?

An undivided heart is not just loyal or focused. It is *consistent*, not saying one thing and doing another, not acting 'out of character'. Faith and works hold together. The contradiction is when we separate them, one from another, dividing them into this and that, when they are designed to be a unity. There should be consistency between who we are (and who we are called to be) and what we do and say.

James makes a distinction between wisdom that is 'from above' and 'earthly' wisdom ('of the devil'). There is a sharp divide here, and the two cannot co-exist – at least, not without disintegration of the heart, not without being tossed about on shifting tides. 'Earthly' wisdom is characterised by selfishness and 'where you have envy and selfish ambition, there you find disorder and every evil practice' (3:13-18). Envy and selfish ambition – desire gone wrong, again. Unholy motivation, inconsistent with our heavenly calling.

If our motives are self-based and confused, we are weakened and our vision is dimmed. We strike out against unforgiving gusts of our own making, running hither and thither as the wind blows. Our desires become straitjackets; we have divided ourselves into boxes, and we cannot understand how we could ever unite our hearts.

We need something beyond ourselves, a strength greater than what we possess, grace to ease the pieces of our hearts together again and focus them on one incredible reality.

> *Where have I been looking,*
> *out upon the shifting sea?*
> *What have I been wanting...*
> *and what have I been asking?*
> *God of grace, help me draw near.*
> *Purify my heart.*

In the first half of this book, we've dipped our toes into the questions of what makes us who we are and what motivates our actions. It's time to strike out further. Now, we're going deeper into the biblical narrative, asking what has motivated God's people, both past and present, looking ahead to our future hope in God's grand salvation story.

REFLECT

- What are the areas of inconsistency in your life?
- James talks about the shifting sea to describe a spiritual reality; Elijah describes the Israelites as 'limping'. In my first chapter, I described letting go of the harness as I abseiled down a church tower. What analogy would you use to describe your life of faith?

Part III

Prizes and
Crowns

Chapter 11
Cause and effect

They will be my people, and I will be their God.
I will give them singleness of heart and action,
so that they will always fear me for their own good
and the good of their children after them.
Jeremiah 32:38-39

Do one thing and it can cause another thing to happen. An action creates a reaction. A single thing can multiply. There may only be one crack in the glass, but it can, ultimately, cause the whole thing to shatter. A seed is sown. If the conditions are right, it takes root and grows into a plant.

Once our brains have developed to a certain point, the question we ask in childhood is that ever recurring 'why'? Many of us, if we're honest, never stop asking it.

Fascination with cause and effect is found in the earliest of humanity's tales, both in the Judeo-Christian narrative and in the stories of other religions and ideologies. We have always sought reasons, wanted to understand the way things are and how they began.

In the great poem of Genesis 1, we read of seed-bearing plants (vv.11-12). Creation is not just brought into being but set into motion. Within its heart is potential for the future. These aren't just plants but plants which yield *seeds*.

In Genesis 2 the first humans are placed in a green space, full of these seed-yielding plants and fruit-bearing trees. This is remembered as humanity's squandered garden, marked by a choice which led to the 'knowledge of good and evil'. Adam and Eve took fruit from the tree of that name, disobeying the one rule of the garden, and thus were barred from the other named tree in the story, the Tree of Life.

Cause and effect.

Covenant clauses

The biblical witness sees creation-wide cause and effect in terms of humanity's relationship with God and with each other. After the Eden story comes the tale of two brothers, in which one murders the other out of jealous rage and thus becomes a 'fugitive and wanderer on the earth' (Genesis 4:3-15).

In the story of the great flood, when God perceives the wickedness of humanity, he decides to destroy all he has made. All except Noah and his family (and those animals too, of course!). When Noah steps off the ark onto dry land, God makes a covenant with him and with *every living creature*. God promises that he will never again flood the whole earth. The sign of this covenant is the rainbow (Genesis 9:8-17).

Later God makes another covenant, with a man called Abram, renamed Abraham because he will be the 'ancestor of a multitude of nations'. Again, it is God who makes the promise. The *sign* of this covenant is circumcision, which is the requirement God makes of Abraham and his descendants, to mark them as God's people (Genesis 17).

Abraham's identity is tied up with *blessing*. The promise is that he will be blessed, that his descendants will share in this blessing and that the nations that spring from them will be *a blessing to the world*. This is a grand vision of cause and effect, beyond the sight of Abraham and Sarah.

Fast forwarding through the years, as Abraham settles, has children and grandchildren; as his grandson Jacob is dubbed Israel; as one of his great grandsons, Joseph, is taken to Egypt, eventually joined by his family, who multiply; as Pharaohs rise and fall and Abraham's descendants are taken into slavery, we reach the time of the exodus from Egypt. This is no longer an individual or family, but a nation. This is the great rescue of Israel, when God calls Moses.

Through Moses, God leads them out of Egypt; to Moses, God gives the Law.

In this law God promises blessing to his people, if they obey his commandments.

If God's people flaunt the Law and disregard God's promise? Then the terms stipulate that instead of receiving abundant blessing, they experience curse.

Cause and effect. Do good, obey God = blessing. Do evil, disobey God = curse.

The Old Testament worldview sees blessing expressed in peace and prosperity. The ideal is a long and prosperous life here and now.

It centres on the provision of land, property, descendants, good health and long life. This blessing is tangible and often material, evident in the lives of those so blessed. Hence, curse means loss of land, lack of descendants, poor health, disease and death, poverty and homelessness. As it did in their wider cultural climate, such things were seen as being 'out of favour' with the divine.

When the formula fails

> *O Lord, why do you cast me off?*
> *Why do you hide your face from me?*
>
> Psalm 88:14

The Old Testament is a multi-coloured volume. The books within it explore life in different ways: they tell stories, recount events, focus on key characters. They include poetry, song, prophecy and wisdom.

Wisdom and folly are often couched in cause and effect terms. The wise choice leads to benefit, the foolish decision to destruction. Proverbs is full of cause and effect, of opposites, of what happens when: pithy little sayings, many of them expressing a righteous/ wicked and wisdom/folly formula, to inspire wise living and bring blessing through it.

But despite these formulae, in the pages of the Old Testament we still find *blips*, when it seems that the 'wicked' are blessed and the 'righteous' suffer. These contrary voices are often found in what is called 'wisdom literature'.[24]

One of them is the writer of Ecclesiastes.[25] 'There are righteous people who perish in their righteousness,' he says, 'and there are wicked people who prolong their fate with evil doing.' (Ecclesiastes 7:15) He sees no distinction in the destiny of all creatures:

> *Surely the fate of human beings is like that of the animals; the same fate awaits them both: As one dies, so dies the other. All have the same breath; humans have no advantage over animals. Everything is meaningless.*
>
> Ecclesiastes 3:19 (NIV)

[24] Job, Ecclesiastes, Proverbs, Song of Songs and some of the Psalms are described in this way. Wisdom literature is a genre that often explores difficult questions. It observes and learns from creation, thinking about the way things are and wondering why they should be so.

[25] Tradition has understood this to be Solomon. The book introduces him as 'teacher' (Qoheleth), 'the son of David and king in Jerusalem' (Ecclesiastes 1:1).

The writer ponders life as he sees it, exploring questions of existence, culminating in a general feeling that everything is 'meaningless'. This has also been translated as 'vanity'. The Hebrew word means something like 'vapour', which ties in with another phrase the writer uses – 'chasing after the wind'. There is a sense of futility, of nothing to grasp, of the insubstantial.

He perceives that we all die – a vague, shadowy end. Why bother stressing about it? It's all… meaningless. As a book, Ecclesiastes (despite the occasional exhortation to enjoy life while we can) can feel bleak. But it shows us the need for nuance in our belief systems; it warns us of being too reliant on a formula-based faith. We do well not to discount the voices which seem jarring to our worldviews.

He's not the only one.

One of the Psalmists claims:

> All this has come upon us,
> yet we have not forgotten you,
> or been false to your covenant.
> Our heart has not turned back,
> nor have our steps departed from your way,
> yet you have broken us in the haunt of jackals,
> and covered us with deep darkness.
> Psalm 44:17-19

We have *not* forgotten you. We have *not* been false. Our heart has *not* turned back…

Yet, you have broken us…

In this Psalmist's opinion, the hearts of the people are still facing the right direction. So… why? *Haven't we fulfilled your conditions? Why is the formula not working? Why doesn't X equal Y?*

The Bible doesn't tend to focus on the general question of why God allows suffering. But its writers ask the more specific variation: 'Why do *good* people suffer'?[26] This is made more pressing for those whose worldview is that all things come from God. The implication for Old Testament writers is that God *sends* suffering, not just that God allows it.

The biblical poets and songwriters look for reasons for their current circumstances; they try to apply a cause-and-effect formula, just as we want to in our circumstances, too.

The question is still 'why?'.

[26] This may be what some people mean when they ask the broader question today.

Why suffering?

It grieves us when one person suffers as the result of another's harmful actions. We recognise the cause and effect principle at work, but it troubles us. It also seems to us that someone can suffer for no reason at all. That troubles us even more.

In the book of Job, the writer/editor sets the stage for exploring this challenge; 'Satan', the accuser in the heavenly court, makes his claim: God's followers are only faithful because they have such comfortable lives. Without the rewards, they would renounce God. It's in their best interest to serve God.

Job becomes a testing ground for this theory. He loses all the factors that made him appear 'blessed' – his position, his property, his health, even his children.

He himself expresses the accepted formula: 'Does not calamity befall the unrighteous and disaster the workers of iniquity?' (Job 31:3) But it doesn't seem to apply.

How can God allow suffering for such a good person as Job? Why does God allow him to be so 'tested'? What can possibly merit such devastation? This is a person described as 'blameless and upright'! (1:8; 2:3)

This question is not answered, at least not by rigorous apologetics or reasoned argument. Here these tools fall down, unable to account for such horrendous suffering. Voices join Job on the stage, suggesting that there is some sin Job has not confessed, somehow causing this to happen. They try to impose a formula, but they fail. The 'friends of Job' are given short shrift at the end.

Explanation or encounter?

How do we deal with this reflection on the harder questions of reality? Job's fortunes are restored, but we struggle to deal with the extent of his former loss. Initially Job declares: 'The Lord gave and the Lord has taken away, blessed be the name of the Lord' (1:21). Eventually, however, this acceptance is not enough for Job – he has to voice a complaint, he can no longer restrain himself. That verse, so often quoted, is only the *beginning* of Job's struggle, not the resolution – which only comes with a soul-shaking meeting with God.

God grabs the microphone. Rather than delivering an answer, God asks impossible questions. Something about this God-encounter silences Job; he cannot argue with it, he cannot even reach the level of reality that lies behind it.

'See, I am of small account; what shall I answer you?' Job says. 'I lay my hand on my mouth.' (40:4)

Job's story explores something we find confusing. Our questions are left hanging; the loose ends remain untied; horrific things happen to good people – here in the pages of our Bible.

This may frustrate us. We try to pin it down, explain it, label it. But the Bible is both 'God-breathed' and human-made. The grappling of the human with the divine is part of the journey we all make; the history of God and humanity is played out on its pages but also on the tender stages of our lives, with all their celebrations and calamities.

We are left with *encounter* – encounter with a God who does not answer all our questions but is God, nonetheless. Are we prepared to encounter such a God as this? And what effect might such an encounter have on us?

Crossing the divide

To Abraham a promise was made of land and descendants, a people belonging to God.

Moses was given laws for living in this promised land. Within this were conditions for the people to obey, including atonement rituals for when the people fell short of their calling.

Later still, David was promised an everlasting kingdom.

Now Jesus is seen as the 'seed' of Abraham, the fulfilment of the Law, our great high priest, the eternal King of David's line. All covenants and promises interweave into this person, one who has become for us both wisdom *and* righteousness (see 1 Corinthians 1:30).

In Jesus, history took an astounding turn, flipping reality on its head, not answering our questions but getting inside them and wearing their clothes. God became flesh, God suffered with us, in Jesus.

Our questions are met with a response like no other. In loneliness and weariness; in pain and anguish; in nails and spear; in blood and water.

The promised messiah is crucified. In the biggest blip of all, God curses himself so that we can be free. 'For our sake he made him to be sin who knew no sin, so that in him we might become the righteousness of God' (2 Corinthians 5:21).

'God is in heaven, and you upon earth,' advised the writer of Ecclesiastes, 'therefore let your words be few' (5:2). But now God *crosses* the heaven-earth divide.

We are blessed with an encounter of which Old Testament writers could not conceive.

This was a defining event, a key in the jail door turning, the chains dropping and yet *still* we 'pick up our cross' and follow. The suffering isn't over yet. It just takes on a different meaning. There's an end in sight, a journey to be taken. The picture of blessing found in the New Testament is rather different from the Old Covenant reality, although sometimes we forget, and want life to fit the old formula (even though, as we've seen, it was never quite that simple).

We still chafe at life's apparent unfairness; we still object to suffering; we still get confused. Our motivation and our sense of meaning need to be based in something beyond these questions, as powerful as they are, in order to live as image bearers. We don't find answers, exactly, but a sense of something beyond words. Something like wisdom, which makes our hearts and minds sensitive to a greater reality. Something like faith, which, though shaken, does not fail.

The challenge of the New Testament is greater than the Old – we are to expect suffering, rejoice in it, even. Our journey, full of question and encounter and puzzlement and pain and joy, is not over yet.

Held in this New Covenant is a heart-deep promise, a deeper motivation than the Law. This is the one that calls for a law 'written on our hearts', of hearts turned from stone to flesh, of God giving his people 'an undivided heart'. This was transformation from the inside out.

> There is so much I do not understand,
> so much I cannot yet grasp.
> I ask for faith, to hold me fast;
> I ask for hope, to lead me on;
> I ask for love, to be my goal.

REFLECT

- What 'formulas' do you ascribe to within your life?
- What questions trouble you?
- Have you ever sought an explanation, only to be confronted instead with an encounter?

Do nothing from selfish ambition or conceit,
but in humility regard others as better than yourselves.
Let each of you look not to your own interests,
but to the interests of others.
Let the same mind be in you that was in Christ Jesus,

who, though he was in the form of God,
did not regard equality with God
as something to be exploited,
but emptied himself,
taking the form of a slave,
being born in human likeness.
And being found in human form,
he humbled himself
and became obedient to the point of death –
even death on a cross.
Philippians 2:3-8

Chapter 12
Deep motivation

We love because he first loved us.
1 John 4:19

To suffer willingly for your faith requires something heart-deep. To care so much for something that you sacrifice for it demonstrates a great depth of love. Jesus did this on the cross. *Greater love has no one...*

Love is the motivator behind the New Covenant but, as we reflect on this, we should recognise that it was also supposed to be the motivator behind the Old. The Law was always meant to be deeper than surface requirements.

Behind the Law
Turn my heart to your decrees...
Psalm 119:36

To focus only on the rituals and external requirements of the Law was to miss the point. The ceremonies of atonement were a form of provision for failure, not a magic wand. They were an allowance, an act of grace. To see them as a way of 'getting away with it' would make a mockery of the whole-life Law. The Israelites were called to *love* God with heart and soul and strength. This was to be their deep motivation.

Jesus himself confronted the ardent law abiders of his time with a frosty accusation – *hypocrites!* What they were on the inside did not correlate with how they looked on the outside (Matthew 23:27-28).

The Law expressed God's love for God's people, God's ownership of them, God's redemption of them when they escaped Egypt. The writer of Psalm 119 waxes lyrical about the Law; he sees it as God's gift, as God's word on his lips, even within the face of suffering: 'My soul clings to the dust; revive me according to your word' (v.25). Things aren't hunky-dory, but he clings to

God's word. For the Psalmist, it's not something empty or 'on the surface' – it goes deep and is full of meaning. 'Oh, how I love your Law!' (v.97)

Lesser motives make for shallow observance, not deep loyalty. The Law itself could not motivate the people if they had no real reverence nor concern about the One who had given it. Something needed to be internalised, the reasons for the Law ingested into the people. If it became an external apparatus, if it was seen merely as a formula for a good life, it was not enough to transform the hearts of the people.

That was the promise of the covenant-to-come:

I will give them an undivided heart and put a new spirit in them;
I will remove from them their heart of stone and
give them a heart of flesh.
Ezekiel 11:19 (NIV)

The new covenant is formed by sacrifice, but instead of hewing an animal in two, as happened when God made the promise to Abraham, the triune God is hewn.

A dangerous calling

He was in the world,
and the world came into being through him;
yet the world did not know him.
John 1:10

Paul describes the Law as a guardian, a custodian of God's people until the coming of Christ (Galatians 3:24). The Law was not the end-game which, having failed, was replaced by Jesus as 'plan B'. The Law was needed until the time was ready for Jesus to be made known to us.

When that time came, Jesus was rejected by those who should have recognised him.

Jesus' motivation went deep into the heart of God. He focused on doing his Father's will. This-earth rewards, pleasant as they can be, could not compete with such a calling.

When Jesus was anointed with the Holy Spirit at his baptism, that same Spirit *drove* him into the wilderness where he was tempted by the devil. The devil's temptations were earth-bound. Jesus had been fasting for forty days and forty nights; he was 'famished'. Turn the stone into bread, the tempter suggested.

Provide food for yourself. What's the point in going hungry when you could snap your fingers and be fed?

One does not live by bread alone, but by every word that comes from the mouth of God.

Strike one.

Jesus was then taken to the pinnacle of the temple in God's holy city. Throw yourself down, teased the tempter. After all, if you really are the Son of God, the angels will catch you.

Do not put the Lord your God to the test.

Strike two.

In one last attempt, Jesus was shown 'all the kingdoms of the world' from a high mountain. He could have them all, according to the devil; that would be his reward, if only he would 'fall down and worship' the one who tempted him.

Worship the Lord your God and serve him only.

Strike three.

The devil left Jesus. In a neat twist the angels, used as leverage during the second temptation, came to wait on him.[27]

Jesus was tempted by self-provision – *command these stones to become loaves of bread!* He was challenged to prove himself in a great spectacle – *throw yourself down!* And finally he was made an offer – *worship me, not God, and you can have all of this.*

The devil picked on the very identity that Jesus had been confirmed at Jesus' baptism, when the voice from heaven declared 'this is my Son' (Matthew 3:17). The devil even used scripture to trip up the one whom scripture had foretold. Provision, proclamation, possession – all these were on offer.

But Jesus' primary motivation was not for his own needs; it was not to show off how special he was; it was not to settle for earthly rewards at the cost of his heavenly calling.

This calling led him to a hill called Golgotha where, in darkness, Jesus died.

[27] Matthew 4:1-11.

The story doesn't end there, but I'd like us to pause in that place of his suffering, for a moment. Consider what love took him there – not just obedience to and love for his Father but their joint love for us. God one-in-three co-operating in an extraordinary way to bring salvation to a lost world.

God's motivation was love, and that love came with a cost.

For God so loved the world that he gave his only Son...

John 3:16

Those who chose to follow Jesus, those who took his message on, often followed a pattern of suffering. They were equipped to do so because of what they believed; what they had seen and heard; what Jesus had done; and because of the Spirit within them. Paul refuses at one point to be paid for his ministry so that his motives cannot be questioned, even when he did have the right to ask for such provision. In fact, preaching the gospel free of charge seems to be what he sees as his reward. He does it 'for the sake of the gospel, that [he] might share in its blessing' (1 Corinthians 9:12-23).

The first followers of Jesus did what they did for the sake of the gospel and for the sake of those who received that gospel. They were motivated by the *good news* of Jesus.

Inclination and incentive

What motivates us, in our lives? Is it external material reward or something deeper? How effective *are* rewards anyway? And what kind of reward are we talking about?

We hear a lot about 'incentives' – especially in the working world. Incentives to do better, to work harder. What does this mean for us at a soul-deep level? And what happens when we do things only for rewards – a kind of surface obedience, a conditional response in a tick-box world?

Rewards can be helpful for routine things. But if the task becomes all about the reward, creativity can be stifled.[28]

What if the work is its own reward? What if we do something because we want to? What if the inclination *is* the incentive?

[28] Daniel Pink discusses this in depth in his book, *Drive: the surprising truth about what motivates us* (Riverhead Books, 2009; published in the UK by Canongate Books, 2010). Pink highlights psychological experiments which showed that when creative thinking was required, material incentives often hampered the quality of the work instead of improving it.

Something shifts here. The task itself is done for the enjoyment and fulfilment of simply doing it, not because an external reward is on offer. The rewards-driven system is not without flaws. Without something deeper, something more intrinsic, we can stall.

Knowing we will get paid for a job does not necessarily mean we do it well. We might do a good job because it's something we consider worthwhile, or because we want to do the best we can, or for the pride of a 'job well done'. It could be important to our sense of identity.

We might work well because we enjoy it. We might do it out of love for someone else. We might choose a low paid job because it feels like the right thing. We may even feel *called* to do it.

We may also, however, do the bare minimum to get the wage. We meet requirements but find them boring and unfulfilling. We don't care, at a heart-level, about what we're doing. This might be about the nature of the work or something specific to our situation. Whatever it is, we would readily admit that our 'hearts aren't in it'.

Falling in love with the art

After the publication of *Forgetful Heart*, I had a good idea of what to write next. I had two good ideas. I was weighing them up when another idea crept up on me, stealing a little piece of my soul. I recognised the symptoms. Here it is – this book cradled in your hands or saved on your device. It would not be ignored, because my motivation was deeper than just an 'idea for a book'. The desire to write another book wasn't enough, not for me.

In order to write this book, I had to fall in love with it.[29]

If it's just work-with-a-deadline, even with the reward of publication, I can't create at my best. I can put something together, of course. Any professional writer needs to be able to produce competent work, including writing about something they are not particularly interested in. I've done that. I can do a decent job to satisfy an editor. (It helps that I like the act of writing itself, so, actually, I'm not without a deeper motivator even then.)

I have the ability to write a book. However, without some internal desire, some love of the work, it won't be my best, it won't be as creative or as passionate.

Something heart-driven has staying power.

[29] Naturally, this also means I've loathed it on occasion.

If all our motivators are external rewards and 'shoulds' and 'shouldn'ts', we are in danger of stagnating. There is something deeper needed, something that will see us through the times of struggle and even suffering, a powerful motivator which dwells within us, a love that strives for more.

Misapplying the formula

We recognise the need for deep motivation. We also recognise that life can be a struggle, that we encounter inexplicable tragedy, pain and sorrow. Yet some still proclaim that old blessing–curse formula, implying that we should expect earthly reward. What happens when we translate this into contemporary Christianity?

The 'prosperity gospel', as it is known, advocates that we should expect earthly blessings now. We can 'claim' these in faith. This isn't just applied to material possessions but to health and wellbeing. There are some parts of the 'health and wealth' movement that are interesting and not so objectionable.[30] Unfortunately, the idea of material provision (and physical healing) as being our *right* is the most blatant expression of it. This is fraught with problems, not least an ever-present danger of corruption.

We are children of the King so, according to some prosperity teachers, we should look like it. Smart clothes, a nice car, cash to spend – these can all be part of this mindset. This makes me wince (that's an understatement!).

Before I judge too hastily, perhaps I should acknowledge that sometimes we do forget to celebrate the privilege of all that God blesses us with. Maybe I could be bolder in my prayers, more confident in my status as God's child. It's good to ask for God's provision and even to expect it. I *do* believe God provides for us and blesses us. I *do* believe this happens in this life as well as 'the next' – but God's provision is not the same as the world's provision. God is generous and unpredictable.

God can bless us enormously here and now, but this is a broader vision than that of having lots of pennies in the bank (haven't we already acknowledged that we are advised not to pursue riches?).

---

[30] For a balanced reflection on some of the motivators and influencers of this movement, I recommend *Faith, Health and Prosperity*, edited by Andrew Perriman (Paternoster Press, 2003).

The wrong flavour

Rewards *will* be given to those who give things up for Jesus 'in this age', as well as eternal life in the age to come (Luke 18:29-30). These smack of abundant provision, replacing what has been lost, what has been given up. They will be so much more than what we left behind. The implication is that, if you're worried about what you might lose, be assured that God will provide for you in far more wonderful ways than the world provides, or that you could provide for yourself.

However, to emphasise personal wealth as our right tastes *wrong* to me. The flavour doesn't remind me of Jesus, who hung out with the poor and himself possessed little. It doesn't speak to me of sacrifice, something that not only marked the life of Jesus but many of his disciples after him.

A prosperity gospel offers an 'immediate', short-term reward. Consider the difference between 'in [God's] presence is fullness of joy' (Psalm 16:11) and 'God wants to bless your finances'. If we make the latter our motivator, how small, how trivial, how (strangely enough) *unrewarding* and conditional this feels compared to that beautiful first statement.

No, I don't like the taste of it. I want to spit it out.

Shallow motivators don't stand up in moments of struggles and suffering. They don't sustain us. Our roots are not deep enough, we risk being uprooted and left without nourishment. The seasons change; the scorching sun bears down on our waterless state, or the frost of winter creeps in upon our lives.

Unless our motivation is made of deep stuff, we'll never wholeheartedly follow Jesus. If our lives are contingent upon immediate reward, we will soon be disillusioned. And if we are only motivated by material results... how small is our love, how conditional, how fragile! Do we love our partners, our friends, because they give us presents? We are grateful for such gifts, but they are not the reason we love the giver.[31]

Rewards (and punishments) have their limits. Unless the motivation for doing good comes from something deeper than external rules, it becomes legalism or ritualism. What God required of Israel was not just an outward observance of the Law. God wanted their love, their loyalty, the core of their being: their *hearts.* Jesus called his followers to 'take up their cross' – in other

[31] Prosperity gospel advocates might object to my implication here, claiming this is not their primary motivator. However, it's hard to see behind it.

words, to be prepared to lose their lives for him (Luke 9:23-24).

God still wants our hearts – every last inch of them. And the reward on offer is not short-term but farsighted, a hope beyond anything we can describe.

> *Gracious God, your love and generosity*
> *cannot be measured, nor contained.*
> *Let us not become consumed by lesser things.*

REFLECT

- What do you think makes for 'deep' motivation?
- How does Jesus' life inspire your own?
- What 'shallow motivators' or short-term rewards do you find uninspiring?

Do you not know that in a race the runners all compete,
but only one receives the prize?
Run in such a way that you may win it.
Athletes exercise self-control in all things;
they do it to receive a perishable garland,
but we an imperishable one.
1 Corinthians 9:24-25

Chapter 13
Propelled by hope

'Do not be afraid; I know that you are looking for Jesus who was crucified. He is not here; for he has been raised, as he said.'
Matthew 28:5b-6a

Our ideas about the future shape our present living. This could be worry about what will happen, or a fatalistic 'what will be, will be'; we might see the future as full of positive potential or terrifying possibilities. What do we think it will be? Where do we plan to go? Even *not caring* about the future has an impact on how we live now.

Our perceptions of the future shift, as we live our lives and collect new experiences. We may (hopefully) become wiser. We are exposed to different viewpoints, for good or for ill. We encounter new influencers, be they situations or people. We may find ourselves growing more optimistic or less. We may become aware of time running out – this can cause panic and paralysis, or a sensation of 'it's too late now' – conversely, it might spur us into action.

We might think we have all the time in the world.

The future affects us in numerous ways – even if it is only an imagined future. But what we believe about the future will affect *the way we live now*.

Jesus was crucified, pierced, laid in a tomb. But he did not stay there.

In the resurrection of Jesus, something happened that broke open death itself. As Peter proclaimed on the day of Pentecost, 'God raised him up, having freed him from death, because it was impossible for him to be held in its power.' (Acts 2:24) The resurrection – and the hope of it – influences our current reality.

The resurrection paved the way to a better hope. The resurrection sliced through the old patterns of death and repeated sacrifices, proclaiming the old system both fulfilled and annulled. The future would be different.

When all the world waited,
and death held our hope
tightly in its cold embrace,
a sigh whispered across
the sweep of reality.
The sigh grew into a breath,
a gust, then a determined breeze –
and death's grip stuttered –
something is happening.
It's a gale now, a living storm –
under its force, death bursts apart,
fractured stone flies in all directions.
Light explodes from the darkest of places
and life covers
everything.

Recognising the risen Jesus

Jesus said to her, 'Woman, why are you weeping? Whom are you looking for?' Supposing him to be the gardener, she said to him, 'Sir, if you have carried him away, tell me where you have laid him, and I will take him away.' Jesus said to her, 'Mary!' She turned and said to him in Hebrew, 'Rabbouni!' (which means Teacher).

John 20:15-16

The risen Jesus was both familiar and unfamiliar. He revealed himself with a word to Mary Magdalene; in the speaking of her name, she recognised the rabbi she loved.

On the Emmaus road, Jesus walked with two of his disciples. They didn't realise who was speaking to them until he gave thanks and broke bread.[32] It was an action he had made to feed thousands; one he made in the upper room, mere hours before his arrest; an action he had, presumably, performed with his disciples in a myriad of mundane, marvellous moments.

Was it that Jesus in his resurrection body was changed in appearance? Or was there something different going on – a kind of deliberate hiddenness and then unveiling, a picture of a journey from limited knowledge to full understanding?

Continuing in Luke's account, after Cleopas and his companion rushed back to Jerusalem, Jesus then appeared to his gathered

[32] Luke 24:13ff

disciples. They thought he was a ghost, even though he had already 'appeared to Simon'. In their worldview, a physical body could not just materialise. Jesus responded to their fear and disbelief by saying: 'Touch me and see; for a ghost does not have flesh and bones as you see that I have.' His body was *corporeal* – it had substance. He then ate some fish to reassure them further.[33]

In John's gospel, we're told of Thomas – poor, heartbroken Thomas – who wanted to follow Jesus anywhere, but had missed seeing his risen Lord. How would that feel? He was already living with the fact that he who had said he would die with Jesus (see John 11:16) had, instead, fled like all the others. So deep-set was his grief and incredulity that he refused to listen to the others proclaiming they had seen the Lord: 'Unless I see the mark of the nails in his hands, and put my finger in the mark of the nails and my hand in his side, I will not believe.'

These are the words of a grieving man. I dislike the term 'doubting Thomas' – for he was not the only disciple to display doubt in Jesus. Jesus, all grace, met him on his terms, offering his wounds for Thomas to touch – but in that moment all Thomas can do is fall at Jesus's feet, proclaiming: 'My Lord and my God!'[34]

Such is the worship engendered by an encounter with the risen messiah. We remember Thomas by his doubt, but he has such a stunning line in the story – *My Lord and my God.*

No longer just his Lord. His God.

There is another account in John, a beachside encounter where, again, the disciples do not initially realise who it is they are seeing. Jesus is recognised in the act of provision – a catch of fish, where they had previously caught nothing. 'It is the Lord!' Peter yells, jumping out of the boat and splashing to shore – although he does pause to put some clothes on first![35]

We may grieve, like Mary, as we search for our living Christ, then find him standing next to us, calling our names. Like those on the road to Emmaus, we can have our eyes unveiled, our hearts set aflame, Jesus revealed to us.

We may not 'see' as Thomas did, but we are called to a deeper belief in our resurrected Lord. We learn from Jesus' response to Thomas: 'You believe because you have seen. Blessed are those who believe but have not seen…' (John 20:29, NIV)

We can splash through the waves as Peter did, delighted when

[33] Luke 24:36-43
[34] John 20:25-28
[35] John 21:1-14

we recognise our Lord. This Jesus – this crucified and risen Jesus – is the true definer and motivator of our lives, calling us from death into life.

A new path

If Christ has not been raised, your faith is futile and you are still in your sins. Then those also who have died in Christ have perished. If for this life only we have hoped in Christ, we are of all people most to be pitied.

1 Corinthians 15:17-19

Resurrection was not a new idea. Many Jews, including the Pharisees, believed in a final resurrection, when the dead will be raised and judged.[36]

We hear Martha attesting to belief in this final resurrection as Jesus approaches the tomb of Lazarus. Jesus' response? '*I am* the resurrection and the life.' (John 11:25, emphasis mine)

What comes through in the New Testament is that Jesus' own resurrection set something extraordinary in motion. He not only patterned humanity as it should be, but humanity as it *will* be for those who are in Christ. Jesus broke the power of death, not just for himself, but for *us*. The Christian hope is not just based around the extraordinary event of Jesus' resurrection, but our own.

This is our future hope.

Belief in the resurrection and in what it meant was the motivating force behind the earliest Christians. Without it, their faith didn't mean anything, because they were still 'in [their] sins' (1 Corinthians 15:17). In crucifixion, chains of darkness had encased Jesus, their messiah. In resurrection, those chains were shattered. A new path was made available. Jesus demonstrated the pattern of life to come.

In the resurrection, Jesus goes ahead of us. We don't just look back at Jesus' resurrection, we *look towards our own*. This is part of the gospel message to us. There is life beyond this. Life that death can't hold. Enduring life. Life given by God, not earned by us.

Without Jesus' resurrection, Christianity would be in vain, because it was in the resurrection that he triumphed over sin and death. Only after Jesus was raised and then 'returned' to his Father, came that vast Spirit-anointing which gave life to his church.

---

[36] See Daniel 12:2. The Sadducees, however, did not believe in a final resurrection (see Matthew 22:23).

Vindication

We cannot leave our faith at the cross, nor linger inside the tomb. What Jesus did does not make sense – or at least, does not achieve its purpose – unless we remember the stone that has been rolled away. The resurrection of Jesus underscores everything that was 'finished' at the cross. It is vindication; it is how we know that death is not the end, that Christ has opened up a new and glorious reality, that death has been 'swallowed up in victory'.

Because of the resurrection, we have the Spirit, sent by the ascended Jesus. It was a step-by-step process, with each part an essential piece of Jesus' story – his incarnation, growing and living among us, death for us, resurrection, ascension, the outpouring of the Spirit (which happened at Pentecost) and the Spirit's indwelling of Christ's body, the church.

There is much blessing to be known in our present lives, as God's reign creeps in, as we are given the privilege of knowing God better and better. But that knowledge is not yet complete. Our hope propels us forward into the future, through drudgery and darkness and even persecution, as many of Jesus' followers experience around the globe. What keeps them going? Why do they cling to this belief, if it causes so much pain and opposition? If there is no final resurrection, Paul writes to the Corinthians, 'why are we putting ourselves in danger every hour? ... If the dead are not raised, "Let us eat and drink, for tomorrow we die".' (1 Corinthians 15:30,32) We might as well focus on enjoying ourselves here and now.

The resurrection hope strengthens us in our struggles for the gospel. It makes us farsighted, for the landscape is suddenly so much richer, so much more promising, so much more enduring.

An imperishable reality

While we are still in this tent, we groan under our burden, because we wish not to be unclothed but to be further clothed, so that what is mortal may be swallowed up by life.

2 Corinthians 5:4

As the 'first fruits' of the resurrection and 'firstborn' from the dead, Jesus goes before us, intercedes for us, demonstrates to us not only what we should be but what we *will* be.[37]

Jesus held things in his risen hands, offered Thomas the opportunity to touch his wounded side – a wound he apparently

[37] See 1 Corinthians 15:20-23; Colossians 1:18; Revelation 1:5

still carried with him. He broke bread, ate fish on a beach, claimed firmly that he was not a ghost. This was different. He was not disembodied; he was very clearly *bodied*!

Often we can portray the 'spiritual' as being insubstantial. But the picture of our future hope is of a strong, blazing, *tangible* reality. Such is the promise of the final resurrection, for us still to come, at the end of the age. Our resurrected bodies will be imperishable, not subject to decay.

In 1 Corinthians 9, Paul tells his readers to 'run in such a way as to get the prize' (v.24, NIV). Look, he says, at how prize winners run! The athletes in the games run to get a temporary crown, or garland, that withers and fades. But we do it for an eternal, lasting crown.

When biblical writers use the metaphor of a crown, something about it bestows a characteristic, or status, to the wearer (usually in the context of future hope, reward and promise). *The crown says something about the wearer or who the wearer will be.*

What this crown confers is not 'perishable' or 'corruptible' (the latter is the word used here) but 'imperishable' and 'incorruptible'. This is similar language to that Paul uses to describe our resurrection bodies in 1 Corinthians 15. What awaits us is something everlasting.

We race towards this – towards complete re-creation, all things made new, towards the eternal not the temporary, that which does not fade or wither or decay – for death will be swallowed up in victory.[38] This is made possible for us by Christ's glorious resurrection.

King of kings,
you demonstrate resurrection life
and sow in me the seeds of the imperishable.
Lift up my head and help me
to perceive a hint of your glory
and a taste of my own future.

REFLECT
- Have you ever got stuck at the empty tomb?
- What encounters have you had with the risen Jesus?
- How does the idea of your future hope motivate you?

[38] See also Philippians 3:14; 1 Peter 1:4; 1 Corinthians 15:54

Do not be deceived;
God is not mocked,
for you reap whatever you sow.
If you sow to your own flesh,
you will reap corruption from the flesh;
but if you sow to the Spirit,
you will reap eternal life from the Spirit.
So let us not grow weary in doing what is right,
for we will reap at harvest time,
if we do not give up.
So then, whenever we have an opportunity,
let us work for the good of all,
and especially for those of the family of faith.
Galatians 6:7-10

Chapter 14

Only the workers

...we know that the one who raised the
Lord Jesus will raise us also with Jesus,
and will bring us with you into his presence.
Yes, everything is for your sake, so that grace,
as it extends to more and more people,
may increase thanksgiving, to the glory of God.
2 Corinthians 4:14-15

We work towards our future hope; our prizes and crowns are not made of temporary stuff. But there are many passing things that tempt us and motivate us, not least attention and admiration from others.

Jesus says that once an earthly reward has been sought and praise given, that's all the reward the show-offs get. It's a short-term goal and a short-term result. Jesus contrasts this with the idea of a reward from God. To do something *without seeking human praise* is far more laudable, and God, the Father of all, 'who sees in secret' will reward you. That reward will mean much more, be much more, than a smattering of earthly applause.[39]

Frankly, a 'well done' from God is a much better reward than a 'well done' from the person down the road.

But sometimes we don't act like it.

Pedestals and praise

We are not trying to please people but God,
who tests our hearts.
1 Thessalonians 2:4

Are we always seeking the approval of others? Do we set ourselves up so that our 'good deeds' are seen? Do we try and clock up as many praise points as possible, as if life were some huge computer

[39] See Matthew 6:1-4

game in which we gain a point for each action, then cash in for a nice gush of approval? As we saw in chapter eight, we live in a world where we can be 'liked' constantly. We are encouraged to share everything. Where is the line between sharing good news with friends and broadcasting success to followers?

God sees our motives. We can pretend. We can even fool ourselves. But if we do something for our own fame or success in the eyes of the others, God knows.

There's a difference between encouraging someone and 'talking them up', but the lines get blurred sometimes. Do you get fluttery in the presence of the famous? Why?

Do we announce a visiting preacher with enormous fanfare, when the person in question would much prefer just a short explanation of who they are and a friendly welcome? Have we begun to embrace worldly ideas of achievement, judging people by their fame, their publishing successes or their frequency on festival line-ups?

Encouraging and affirming someone's ministry is very important. Paul praises his companions throughout his letters. He is effusive about them and often commends them, but emphasises the need to seek Christ's approval alone. Cheering someone on and acknowledging their value in your eyes is not a bad thing. But I think we can detect when it becomes more of an announcement of an entertainer, listing all their achievements and focusing on their notoriety, as opposed to showing genuine interest in their lives, appreciation for the impact they've had on us and giving them a warm, encouraging welcome.

We get tangled up with our celebrity culture. It helps no one. Consider 'famous Christians' who have disappointed their 'followers' because they messed up. They fell off the pedestal, to great condemnation. Yes, teachers are to be judged more strictly[40] – but by God, I think, not us – and how high that pedestal was! Should they have been up there in the first place?

We forget that they are all only workers… in someone else's field.

Fields and buildings

What then is Apollos? What is Paul? Servants through whom you came to believe, as the Lord assigned to each. I planted, Apollos watered, but God gave the growth.

[40] See James 3:1

So neither the one who plants nor the one who waters is anything, but only God who gives the growth. The one who plants and the one who waters have a common purpose, and each will receive wages according to the labour of each. For we are God's servants, working together; you are God's field, God's building.

1 Corinthians 3:5-9

The believers in Corinth had split into factions, claiming to follow Paul or Apollos or simply Christ (the third hardly seems bad, but in this divisive environment the groups seem to have set themselves against each other).

Paul's response and premise are simple: one may sow, another may water, but God makes things grow; God *owns* the field.

Paul and Apollos merely work for God. They plant and water the field that is owned by God, which is the church. They are fellow workers, helping provide the right conditions and thus acting as conduits for growth – but they do not make things grow. Only God does that.

By 'creating a following' around the workers, the Christians in Corinth missed the point; they looked away from the source of their growth and in doing so endangered their own journeys of discipleship. Their motivation got all tangled up with personality politics and human loyalties rather than hearts and minds fixed on God.

Paul also uses a building analogy, describing himself as a master builder, laying a foundation, with someone else building on it. He and Apollos are both builders, but the foundation itself is Jesus Christ – the only foundation that can be laid and the only thing that we can be certain of remaining.[41]

The builders' work will be judged by its quality. Some materials are destroyed by fire; others are purified and remain strong. Wood, hay, straw – these are all combustible elements. The work of the builders remains if it is of eternal value, but is destroyed if it can't stand the heat! For those whose work survives, there will be a reward. The nature of the reward is not specified, but Paul makes clear that there is a difference between this judgement of works and the salvation of the builders, who are saved 'as through fire' – by the skin of their teeth, we might say.[42] The works don't hold up, so they are lost.

---

[41] 1 Corinthians 3:10-11
[42] The phrase 'by the skin of one's teeth' is suggested by Anthony C. Thiselton in *1 Corinthians: A Shorter Exegetical & Pastoral Commentary* (Eerdmans, 2006) p.66.

It's foolish to make saviours out of the builders. Their work has not even been judged yet!

Paul and his companions are to be regarded as servants of Christ, entrusted as stewards with the secret things of God. This is a privilege. They will be proven trustworthy – or not – by God alone. 'I do not even judge myself,' Paul says, telling his readers that they should 'not pronounce judgement before the time, before the Lord comes, who will bring to light the things now hidden in darkness and will disclose the purposes of the heart'.[43]

By acting as fans rather than friends, those in the church hinder the workers and their work rather than glorifying God. No one is helped by it. It all gets mixed up with human expectation, success and disappointment.

Expectation versus encouragement

I asked for help;
you gave me heartache.
I asked for assistance,
but was met by expectation.
I asked to be real;
you demanded a hero.

The assumption that someone will always succeed can be discouraging, even crippling. Think of the student who 'always' gets straight As, undergoing tremendous mental and emotional strain because of the pressure to maintain the grades. Think of the person who says, meaning all things good, 'You'll do great,' followed by the terrifying: 'You always do'.

You always do? We may make this judgement based on successful past performance, but circumstances can change and people may still feel ill-equipped for a task. If we judge others like this, we unwittingly make it all about them, because they are the ones who are always wonderful, brilliant, the ones who 'always pull it off'. They have a special kind of magic – and this magic is assumed for all future endeavours.

This expression of a fixed mindset (for surely that is what it is) leaves no room for error, and should it *not* go well, adds another bell toll to their despair. 'You always do,' leads to the question screaming within: 'what if I *don't*?'.

The way we say things matters.

[43] 1 Corinthians 4:1-5

'I'll be rooting for you,' is different. 'We're in it with you,' gives strength. 'We're all cheering you on,' is encouragement, not assumed perfection. 'Whatever happens, we care. God loves you.' *That's the way to do it.*

The key to encouragement is not to tell others that they are perfect, as that will never hold water, but to meet them in their worries and assure them of your love. Affirming someone is not the same as over-praising them. Encourage, but don't assume that someone will do well just because they have before. *Make sure they know that your love is not dependent on their success.*

The friends we need

Therefore encourage one another and build up each other, as indeed you are doing. But we appeal to you, brothers and sisters, to respect those who labour among you, and have charge of you in the Lord and admonish you; esteem them very highly in love because of their work.

1 Thessalonians 5:11-13a

In the light of this, how do we approach the workers and their work? Do we constantly rave about them in the eyes of others, or do we focus on bringing them down? Both are harmful. Yes, they are 'only the workers', but God cares about them; so should we. They are dealing with stresses and difficulties about which we may have no clue. Our support is essential to their wellbeing. We're called to build one another up, to love and encourage each other. But how do we voice this encouragement?

To be the person someone has 'pedestalised' can be horribly hard work and leave no room for real self-reflection or spiritual engagement. All that person is left with is a sense of the cavernous difference between how they are perceived and what they know about themselves. Their weaknesses loom large; feelings of inadequacy can overwhelm them. If they ever struggle with temptation or stubborn sin-stains on their hearts, it's harder to confess such things. Their context is not one of support and sustenance but admiration and expectation.

We are to be friends and supporters, not fans and admirers. Our calling is neither to puff others up, nor break them down, but to be the ones to whom they can turn in times of weakness or need.

We are called to *love* them.

Let's not make a hobby of putting people on pedestals, but let's not make a hobby of 'knocking them off', either. Let's act with compassion and gentleness towards one another. Do we constantly criticise, playing our games of 'spot the speck' (in your eye)? Do we know the power of our words to belittle, to destroy, to break a person's heart?

Encouragement is a powerful thing, but discouragement can be even more so. Encouragement keeps momentum going; lack of it makes effort feel harder. But discouragement? Discouragement can knock us down completely, none more so than when it comes from someone we assumed would be our encourager. Receiving the opposite from these people can strike a blow from which it is hard to recover. Enough blows like this and we can retreat into ourselves; our hopes and dreams diminish; we fall into a state of coping rather than thriving.

Our potential is tender and needs nurturing. When it is dismissed or devalued, it can give up or hide itself away, taking a form which does not have the strength to initiate that which it was made for. To feel stifled in this way can suck all the joy out of a person.

If you feel inclined to 'have a go' at someone, ask yourself – what is *my* motive in all of this? Am I pushing someone down to make *myself* feel more important? Has my desire to get my opinion heard eclipsed the need to be sensitive and constructive? (There are times when criticism is valid but, again, how we say things matters.) Are we doing it to help someone in their journey of faith or just because *we want to get our point across*?

The worth of our work

> ... be steadfast, immovable, always excelling in the work of the
>   Lord, because you know that in the Lord your labour is not
> in vain.
>
> 1 Corinthians 15:58

How do we feel about our own work for the gospel? I think we can gain satisfaction from it, without boasting or bragging. But we need to ask ourselves, when we do something, *why* we are doing it.

We might say we're doing something for God, but here's the test – *if no one else noticed, would we feel put out?* Do we feel obliged to share with everyone all things we've been doing 'for God'? In our testimonies, are we giving praise to God for what God has done, or are we pointing out the amazing things *we've* been doing?

When we start self-pedestalising we are really in trouble, far from any heavenly reward. We become applause junkies, living life on the addictive juice of earthly praise, which is pretty sweet for a while, but will eventually run dry.

Have you felt the weight of expectation in your life? It can get to the point that even when we don't 'feel the feelings', we pretend that we do, because we're not given the space to be honest. We need to ask ourselves: is there someone with whom we can be honest? Someone who will not pedestalise us but hold us to account? Someone who won't sneer at us but will hear our whispers of weakness with compassion and understanding?

We cannot judge the worth of our work – whether dubbing it 'useless' or 'wonderful' – because it is not up to us to judge. We don't see the full picture. *We cannot tell what will endure.*

We don't always see the results of our labours. Our efforts may not seem to bear the fruit we desired, at least, not to our eyes. Our work can seem longwinded, slow in coming to fruition, but God sees all our efforts for him and values them. The fruit may not be the colour or taste we expect, but if God provides the growth, we know that it will be far better than anything we could imagine.

All that we do is done in the grace of God. Our work is not for our own glory but for the glory of the one who gives us life beyond measure. And 'when Christ who is your life is revealed, then you also will be revealed with him in glory' (Colossians 3:4).

We need to remind ourselves: we are only the workers.

God owns the field.

REFLECT

- How do you feel about your own 'work' for God?
- Have you built someone up so much that you cannot imagine them being 'weak'? On the other hand, are you guilty of constant criticism, picking at people, bringing them down (whether to their faces or not)?
- Encouragement, when done in healthy ways, can be a wonderful motivator. Pray for compassion and wisdom to exercise it well.

So if you have been raised with Christ,
seek the things that are above,
where Christ is,
seated at the right hand of God.
Set your minds on things that are above,
not on things that are on earth,
for you have died,
and your life is hidden with Christ in God.
When Christ who is your life is revealed,
then you also will be revealed with him in glory.
Colossians 3:1-4

Chapter 15
What in heaven's name?

*... our citizenship is in heaven, and it is from there
that we are expecting a Saviour, the Lord Jesus Christ.
He will transform the body of our humiliation so that
it may be conformed to the body of his glory, by the power
that also enables him to make all things subject to himself.*
Philippians 3:20-21

In Jesus, we find the promise of eternal life. We work towards an eternal crown. But eternal can be a statement of quality, not just duration, something that smacks of 'the age to come'. To say a reward is eternal does not mean it is future-only!

When we think about future reward, our thoughts often turn heavenwards.

But what *is* heaven?

We're told that heaven is the place of our citizenship, where our inheritance is kept for us, where our treasure should be.[44] Does this make it a kind of divine storage facility? Does heaven have the best 'safe' of them all? Or is it just 'the place we go when we die'?

Pieces of sky

*We play with ideas of eternity
the golden, heavenly kiss
blue skies, ethereal entities
out of focus, soft white wisps –
less solid than all that we know.
But if God is creator of everything,
if heaven truly exists,
wouldn't it be something
far more real than this?*

In our cultural depictions, heaven feels unsubstantial, like cloud city

---

[44] Philippians 3:20; 1 Peter 1:4; Matthew 6:20

(where the Care Bears live). For some, it's a place of personal wish fulfilment – ask them what heaven is like and they'll list the things they love – ice cream or daisies or a favourite celebrity.

Some think it's boring. 'I don't want to sit on a cloud with a harp,' I was informed by a contemporary of mine at sixth-form college. 'I want a bottle of Jack Daniels in my own corner of hell.'

For some, heaven is a place to celebrate, with angels and their party poppers. To others, it seems pale and washed out, plus you need good fingers for all that harp playing. Cloud sitting doesn't seem appealing.

In the Bible, 'heaven' (or 'heavens') sometimes refers to the sky. An old worldview saw the sky as a dome above the earth, holding back the waters.[45] Above this, the ancients believed, was the domain of the divine. The playground of the god(s) was 'up there', while we humans lived 'down here'. 'O that you would tear open the heavens and come down!', we read in Isaiah (64:1). Further down, beneath the grave, was the place of the dead.

This directional language has remained long after scientific discovery has shown us what lies beyond our sky. We would not now use geography to locate God's heaven. Perhaps we might instead say that heaven is another dimension, unseen but close.

The biblical picture of the heaven-where-God-dwells is of a place of blazing glory, filled with the presence of God.

Heaven is God's domain.[46]

Resurrection pending

> Going to heaven! —
> How dim it sounds!
> Emily Dickinson

However, many think mainly of heaven as 'where people go when they die' – or where *some* people go, at least. Many evangelists have begun by asking, 'Do you believe you are going to heaven?' Is this right – to think of heaven primarily as an 'afterlife reality'?

What *does* the Bible say about life after death?

The Old Testament picture of the afterlife is limited – a mysterious, silent place, described as 'Sheol', the Pit and, occasionally, 'Abaddon'. The despairing Psalm 88 contains all three descriptions and asks: 'Are your wonders known in the darkness, or

[45] Hence the 'heavens open', when it rains.
[46] For more on the nature of heaven in the Bible, I recommend Paula Gooder's *Heaven* (SPCK, 2011).

your saving help in the land of forgetfulness?' (v.12) This dark 'land of forgetfulness' is in strong contrast to the vibrancy of earthly life, let alone God's heavenly glory. God cannot be praised by those in 'Sheol'.[47] The Old Testament focuses on seeking long and prosperous earthly lives.

In the New Testament, we find the language of resurrection, eternal life and kingdom. Yes, we see glimpses of heaven. But the term 'going to heaven' is not a biblical phrase.

What *is* there is a promise of a future reality, when all will be made new. What *is* there is a final resurrection and utter defeat of death. What *is* there is a new heaven and new earth, where God will dwell – *on earth* – with his people. According to the Bible, the new eternal reality comprises of a heady mix of both heaven and earth.

Biblical writers are set on the end – the final resurrection and recreation. They don't break down the in-between as much as you may think. Any 'intermediate state' is *resurrection pending.* That future hope remains for all of us, living and dead.

There are tantalising hints of the 'in-between', for those who have died – Paul longs to be 'away from the body and at home with the Lord'. He reassures the Thessalonians that they will be reunited with those who have died (literally 'fallen asleep'). Those who have passed away are still in Christ.[48]

Jesus promised the thief on the cross that he would be with him 'today in paradise'. Revelation pictures multitudes praising God in heaven. Jesus goes to prepare many rooms in his 'Father's house' for his disciples; could these be heavenly sojourns before the final renewing of everything?[49] Whatever this 'in-between' will be, we know that we wait in God's heavenly care for the reality and reunion of Christ's appearing.

But the Bible does not claim heaven to be our *final* destination. Recreation is yet to come – when everything, heaven and earth, is made new.

New beginnings

For the Lord himself, with a cry of command, with the archangel's call and with the sound of God's trumpet, will descend from heaven, and the dead in Christ will rise first. Then we who are alive, who are left, will be caught up in the clouds

[47] See Psalm 6:5; Isaiah 38:18.
[48] 2 Corinthians 5:8; 1 Thessalonians 4:13-17
[49] Luke 23:43; Revelation 7:9-17 (although it's hard to extrapolate times and places from Revelation); John 14:2-3

together with them to meet the Lord in the air; and so we will be with the Lord for ever.

1 Thessalonians 4:16-17

The Lord *descends* to us *from* heaven. Both the living and the risen dead go to meet him. It is a picture of joyous reunion, not a permanent suspension in the clouds. It's not an escapist vision; it's a new, tangible beginning for all of us.

N.T. Wright has written about this metaphor of an emperor returning to his subjects, them going to greet him, and *coming back with him.*[50] (Others see this as a picture of a 'rapture' of believers escaping a coming tribulation. Regardless of your interpretation, the final picture is of an eventual return to the new earth. We don't *stay* 'in the air'.)

In the Bible, death is often depicted as an enemy to be vanquished. Life is a gift to us. Yes, the sting of death will be removed but it has a 'sting' to be removed in the first place.[51] The Bible does not see death as a glorious release from soul from body (as the Platonic worldview might). We don't anticipate drifting about in a permanent body-less state.

Paul says:

Listen, I will tell you a mystery! We will not all die, but we will all be changed, in a moment, in the twinkling of an eye, at the last trumpet. For the trumpet will sound, and the dead will be raised imperishable, and we will be changed. For this perishable body must put on imperishability, and this mortal body must put on immortality.

1 Corinthians 15:51-53

We are destined not for cloud-sitting, but for an embodied, enduring reality. Our inheritance is kept safe in heaven, ready for this new hope.

A diminished gospel

Is Christianity seen as a choice between 'going to heaven' and 'going to hell' when we die? We hold out the carrot (heaven) and brandish the stick (hell). A 'carrot and stick' approach, in general,

[50] For a short summary, see Wright's 2001 article 'Farewell to the Rapture', available to view at www.ntwright.com.
[51] 1 Corinthians 15:54-56

has limited effect on the long-term. If this is the system, we can feel unfulfilled in our lives on earth.

If we have a carrot-and-stick gospel, *we diminish it.*

Is our 'carrot' comprised of a future reality of which we struggle to conceive? Is that what it should be – paradise-in-the-waiting our sole motivation? And then (traditionally anyway), the terrifying stick of hell – 'scaring people into salvation'? The effect of this can lead to a pendulum swing – a kick back against these things because they've been communicated so poorly.

The word most often translated as 'hell' in the New Testament is *gehenna*. This referred to a valley outside the walls of Jerusalem. It was a place where, historically, people – *children* – had been sacrificed to idols. It was a place of broken covenant, associated with judgement.[52]

The place of destruction is usually presented as that which is outside the kingdom of God, not as a precise opposite to 'heaven'. (The kingdom of God is present in heaven, but it's not the same thing, as we will see!) Jesus talked *gehenna* language in the Sermon on the Mount.[53] He emphasised that it wasn't our external appearances that mattered but the thoughts of our hearts – from which our words and actions spring. God sees us in the secret as well as public places.

Warnings about *gehenna* in the New Testament are often directed at the 'in-crowd', rather than being used as an evangelistic tool. Jesus challenged those who abused their position as law makers and teachers. He used the image of *gehenna* to make a profound statement about those who acted without compassion and justice. The shocking description of the fate of those who abused their role as image-bearers would have been appalling to some in Jesus' audience. When Jesus talked about *gehenna*, he often addressed those who had acted against the poor, abused God's people and denied them access to God's kingdom.

[52] Many commentators also say it was the city dump, where rubbish (and the bodies of executed criminals) were burned, although some question the evidence for this, e.g. G.R. Beasley Murray in *Jesus and the Kingdom of God* (Eerdmans, 1986) – in a footnote!

[53] References to being 'outside the kingdom' include fire, outer darkness, weeping and gnashing of teeth. There are also New Testament mentions of 'Hades', a Greek name for the realm of the dead; some carry a sense of judgement or waiting for judgement. In 2 Peter 2, the angels are held for judgement in 'Tartarus'. Revelation talks of a lake of fire and sulphur, the 'second death' and the ultimate destruction of death and Hades. (I can't explore this further here; it's not the focus of this book.)

Life in pictures

Picture language can be helpful – I use it often – but where words and pictures stretch desperately to convey an indescribable reality we should not then necessarily force the reality into the picture. Traditional emphasis on literal fire and brimstone may, ironically, have obscured the profound nature of what Jesus was saying.

The Bible *does* talk about eternal destinies, about what is needed to enter the kingdom of God (more on that later) and the seriousness of what happens to us in the future. It's important to recognise and engage with this, beyond the picture language of light and dark, water and fire. But the Bible is not a list saying 'do this to get into heaven' and 'do this and you'll go to hell'. If we have made the gospel message into that, we've lost its richness. Christianity becomes an escapist 'ticket' to an abstract heaven rather than a transforming, enduring, body-and-soul reality that begins now.

We neglect to convey the thrilling depth of the gospel. In Christ, what was dead is now alive! All will be made new! Perhaps our starting question should be: do you want to live? *Really* live? Do you want to be free, to be loved, to know and explore an extraordinary new reality, that will one day be fully revealed? To be part of God's plans for the present *and* the future?

What about life-with-God? What about fullness of joy? What about looking at the biblical view of heaven, recreation and the new earth where God will dwell with us? I'm not saying that eternal destiny is not important. *I'm saying that it is,* but that we need to flesh out that reality for people with the whole beautiful story of God-with-us – in Jesus, in the Spirit, and finally with the all-powerful triune God dwelling among us for all time.

Citizens of heaven

It can be tempting to see heaven as some 'far-off land', without much relevance to our present lives. However, if we are citizens of heaven, we carry that identity with us now – even if we are not fully experiencing it yet. There is a sense in which we do 'not belong to the world', that we live as 'aliens and strangers'.[54] We are called *out* from the 'world' and its values – as from darkness into light.

Our lives are 'hidden with Christ in God' (Colossians 3:3). When Paul encourages the Colossians to set their minds on things above, he is talking about those things that are *characteristic* of heaven. In accepting Christ, we have already died to what we used to be; our

[54] John 17:14; 1 Peter 2:11

enduring, eternal life is now kept safe for us, until the day it is fully revealed.

Sometimes it's said that we're 'just passing through'; that this is 'not our home'. We recognise the pain and evil in our current world and look towards the time it will be no more. There are Christians in our world who are persecuted for their faith and who hunger, quite rightly, for a different reality. We know that there are values in our world which conflict with values of the kingdom of God.

We inhabit what is temporary; our 'promised land' is still to come. There is a sense of pilgrimage in our lives towards our future hope. We are not to invest in the material and temporary but instead the eternal.

But to say we're 'just passing through' may be a misleading way of putting it.

It can reinforce the idea of our destiny being in a faint and distant heaven, without acknowledging the future hope of our new earth, expressing a wish to 'escape' as individuals rather than be restored as community on a creation-wide scale. It can discourage us from making a difference where we are. Even when the Israelites were in exile they were told to invest in their current community, to 'seek the welfare of the city' where they were in exile (Jeremiah 29:7). Instead of focusing on our 'homesickness' as a way of rejecting our current reality, can it not motivate us to bring more of that fuller reality into our lives now?

We can decorate our lives with markers of our future hope. Our citizenship of heaven and our identity in Christ should infuse, in practical ways, our lives here and now. What we learn about God in this life is not scrapped in the next – in fact all that which witnesses to God and God's eternal reality has staying power. We have heavenly treasures, held safe for us. These are the works that endure.

We are moving towards a better future, but we make a difference – in the present – as we do so.

Beyond our dreaming

We wait for new heavens and a new earth,
where righteousness is at home.
2 Peter 3:13b

Let's talk about knowing God and being known by God; let's talk about eternal life as something that starts now, about living for God *because we love God* and loving God *because God loves us!* If this seems a weak motivation, it's because we've been seduced by a sugar-coated version of love, not the perfect, fierce, uncompromising love of God.

We downgrade heaven in our vague imaginings, forgetting the blazing glory of the heaven-dwelling God. God's judgement is serious stuff, but again has become faintly nonsensical as God is envisioned as a human tyrant rather than a just and loving judge, who can be trusted with our lives, knowing our hearts as completely as God does. We cartoon-ise all of it.

Our pictures become such caricatures that they seem unreal and thus *lose their impact.* We make them into Hollywood versions of reality. They become the stuff of dreams – or nightmares. Inspiring, comforting, frightening or unsettling. But still dreamlike; still impossible to grasp.

How rich is our gospel; how much more than a dream. Let's not trivialise it, diminish it, turn it into 'bumper-sticker' theology, all surface and no depth… *please.*

For the love of God – the extraordinary, beautiful, abounding love of God surrounds us, invites us – *let us enter in.*

Heaven come down

'See, the home of God is among mortals.
He will dwell with them;
they will be his peoples,
and God himself will be with them… '
Revelation 21:3

The God who has already chosen to take on our flesh, to break death from the inside out, is the God who comes again in glory. This God is not slow at promise-keeping, but wants all to repent, to know the wonder of a complete change of direction, a realigning of our hearts.[55]

We model our earthly lives on heavenly ways. We long for reunion with those who are missing – temporarily – from our lives, but kept safe in Christ. We look for the kingdom of God to be revealed. Our call into God's kingdom is an invitation to be part of something glorious.

At the end of this age, as Revelation weaves its image of the Holy City coming 'down' from heaven, *heaven comes to earth;* God's reality and our reality combine.[56]

[55] See 2 Peter 3:9
[56] See Revelation 21:1-4

The fullness of God will dwell on earth.
God really will tear open the heavens and come down.

> *Beloved, we are God's children now;*
> *what we will be has not yet been revealed.*
> *What we do know is this:*
> *when he is revealed, we will be like him,*
> *for we will see him as he is.*
> 1 John 3:2

REFLECT

* What is your idea of heaven?
* Do you think we've turned Christianity into a carrot and stick gospel?
* How can we decorate our lives with tasters of eternity?

Part IV
Children and Heirs

Chapter 16
First things first

The kingdom of the world has become the kingdom of our
Lord and of his Messiah,
and he will reign forever and ever.
Revelation 11:15

Sometimes people take the idea of future recreation to mean we can do anything we like with this present earth. It doesn't matter what car you drive or how many trees you chop down, because, according to their understanding of biblical prophecies, it will all be destroyed, anyway. It's a bit like the 'I'll commit sin because God will forgive me' understanding of grace. It misses the point.

Creation gives us tasters of its creator.[57] Do we dismiss that revelation, shaming God's name by how we treat what God has made? If we fritter away the good things of this creation, treating them as valueless, we're not being good stewards. More than that, we're not witnessing to the future reality of a joy-filled new earth (which has the same creator).

Our mandate to take care of this creation hasn't vanished. We are to be kingdom-dwellers now, because eternal life – the 'age-to-come-life' – is seen, in part, in our present living. You could say that, just as the Old Covenant was a sketch of the New, our current earth is a shadow, a sketch of what is to come.

Jesus pointed towards a new way of living, something that starts now, as well as looking towards the future. One way Jesus talked about this was in the language of *kingdom.*

Pointers and parables
'What shall we say the kingdom of God is like,
or what parable shall we use to describe it?'
Mark 4:30 (NIV)

---

[57] Romans 1:20

The gospel message is an invitation to participate in God's kingdom. What is this kingdom?

The main ways in which Jesus talks about kingdom are through stories and pictures. 'The kingdom of God is like...', Jesus says.[58]

Jesus tells his disciples that the secrets of the kingdom are given to them through parables (Matt 13:10ff). He doesn't give a dictionary definition but a series of tableaux, stories and statements. The Sermon on the Mount is full of them.

The impact of the kingdom is seen as a mustard seed which grows into an enormous tree, as a precious pearl found in a field and as hidden treasure – each worth selling everything in order to get. It's like yeast worked into dough – just a small amount needed to make everything rise. The 'word of the kingdom' is like a seed sown, and the impact depends on the state of the soil.[59]

We need to be *ready*, like the 'wise virgins' in the parable, as they expect the return of the bridegroom, with spare oil at hand to keep our lamps burning. We are to use our resources productively, like those entrusted with 'talents' by their master when he goes away.[60]

In Jesus, the Kingdom comes *near*; therefore we are called to repent of our old ways.[61] The Pharisees once asked him when the Kingdom of God would come. Jesus responded: 'the coming of the kingdom of God is not something that can be observed, nor will people say, "Here it is," or "There it is," because the kingdom of God is in your midst.' (Luke 17:20-21, NIV)

The royal reign of God

The Old Testament expectation of the kingdom was of an earthly one, over which David's descendent would reign, with Jerusalem as its centre. Jesus describes something wider than this, something bound up with Jesus himself. For us, too, the word 'kingdom' can confuse us; we think of a limited geographical area rather than an all-encompassing reality. We might instead describe it as the reign of God. Alister McGrath suggests that 'kingship' might be a good word.[62]

---

[58] Matthew, perhaps in deference to his primarily Jewish audience, usually refers to it as the 'kingdom of heaven'. They are two ways of saying the same thing – it is not a reference to 'going to heaven'.

[59] All these are found in Matthew 13.

[60] Matthew 25:1- 30

[61] Matthew 3:2; 10:7

[62] Alister McGrath, *Christian Theology: An introduction* (Wiley-Blackwell, 4th revised edition, 2006), p.465

The reign of God is something worthwhile and precious beyond belief; it defies expectation and the 'wisdom of the world'. The first is often last and the last first. This emphasis challenged the religious elite who considered themselves the heirs, chosen ones and children of Abraham. Jesus uses shock tactics when he tells them that 'the tax collectors and prostitutes are entering the kingdom of God ahead of you' and that the kingdom of God 'will be taken away from you and given to a people who will produce its fruit.' They are even guilty of 'shutting the kingdom' in people's faces. The original heirs of the kingdom face the prospect of being cast out and other 'heirs' being brought in. It will be given to those who produce 'fruits of the kingdom' rather than those who rejected the one who was sent to them.[63]

You need to be 'like a child to enter the kingdom'. The humble will be the greatest. The kingdom belongs to the poor (and poor in spirit); it is a struggle for the rich to enter. The master who is shown mercy but does not show it himself will be cast out, likewise those who have been forgiven but do not forgive… [64] It turns upside down ideas of who should 'belong', throwing it open to those seen as 'lesser' in the eyes of the elite.

There is an inheritance prepared, but not everyone receives it – the sheep will be separated from the goats (depending on how they treat those suffering from hunger, thirst, nakedness, imprisonment, sickness or those who are strangers); the good fish separated from the bad (the 'righteous' from the 'evil'); likewise the weeds from the wheat.[65]

The righteous requirement

Jesus answered [Nicodemus], 'Very truly, I tell you, no one can see the kingdom of God without being born from above.'

John 3:3

There is a righteous requirement to kingdom living. The 'righteousness' of the Pharisees is not enough; we are to exceed it![66] Jesus thinks little of external displays of righteousness. He looks beyond surface behaviours to thoughts and motives (such as anger and lust). The righteousness Jesus desires is deeper.

[63] Matthew 21:31; 21:43; 23:13; 21:42-44
[64] Matthew 19:14; 18:4; Luke 6:20 (Matthew 5:3); Matthew 19:23; Matthew 18:23-35
[65] Matthew 25:31-46; 13:47-50; 13:24-30
[66] Matthew 5:20

The word in Greek can be translated as 'justice', and we shouldn't divide them into completely different concepts. Justice and righteousness are joined at the hip. If we get caught up in our individual moral purity (as some of the Pharisees may have done) while neglecting the needs of others, *this is not the biblical concept of righteousness.* The righteousness we are to seek *includes* the individual but is not individualistic. How we treat others is fundamental.

'Blessed are those who hunger and thirst for righteousness', who are persecuted for its sake (Matthew 5:6,10). To be a kingdom dweller is not just about keeping our own houses clean but about paying attention to the needs of those around us.

If kingdom is about the royal reign of God, if believers are to live in loving community, then the 'requirements' of living under this reign emphasise how we live together under the kingship of God. We honour God by loving one another, by providing for one another, by remembering those who have little and being generous with our own abundance, by acting with fairness and justice, forgiveness and mercy.

We can only do this by following Jesus, with the help of the Holy Spirit, by being 'born from above'.

Purpose and priority
But strive first for the kingdom of God and his righteousness,
and all these things will be given to you as well.
Matthew 6:3

The seeking of God's kingdom – and God's righteousness – is not an 'also' thing but an 'all' thing. In this passage Jesus talks about survival-type issues. Enough to eat. Clothes to wear. Things we often worry about. These things God will take care of, Jesus says, if we seek the kingdom first. They will fall into place, be given, 'added unto you' (*Ah! Lay! Loo! Yah!*).

What does it mean to give this reality priority? Not always what we expect. The wisdom of God can seem foolish to us. We don't understand it; it up-ends our preconceptions. Likewise, the kingdom can slide between our fingers the minute we make it about what *we* think it should be.

In the kingdom, treasures are found in unexpected places, the poor are considered rich and the weak are made strong. The mark of God's reign is not a king surrounded by worldly-wise (possibly corrupt!) advisers; not a ruler holed up in a palace or a grand house, in front of which people stand taking selfies; not an emperor with all the trappings of riches. Instead it's a movement of peace, righteousness and topsy-turviness, light shining in the dark, preparing for the day when darkness will be destroyed and this movement consumes everything from the inside out.

It can take a bit of practice to tune into this reality, a bit of determined 'seeking' before we can grasp even part of it. We need the Spirit's help in our searching, so that our senses can detect kingdom in the strangest of places and, perhaps, the *lack* of it in places that seem so promising on the surface, but in reality are just full of 'worldly' treasures.

Good news is found here: wholeness for the broken, hope for the despairing, challenge for those who think they've got it made and, yes, judgement for those who abuse their privileges and make it harder for people to find God. Other kingdoms will fall. They have to fall, in the end, so that the true kingdom, heaven-branded stuff, God-shaped living, can permeate everything.

When we seek first the kingdom of God, other necessities will be provided, perhaps in ways we did not expect – nor even approve of – at least, not in our own human wisdom and opinion.

Our present reality
Your kingdom come.
Luke 11:2b

God's royal reign is not yet fully known, but the stamp of it can be seen on those who believe and seek to bring it nearer.

However, sometimes it's hard to spot this stamp. Not only do we feel oppressed and confused by the state of the world, there are Christians arguing about kingdoms and rulers, about right and wrong, even condemning one another. They make baffling choices, idolise money and fame, invest power in the ungodly, ignore the needs of the poor, close doors instead of opening them, focus on short-term goals and not that far-sighted vision.

Where is the kingdom, here?

What about we who are quick to judge and condemn others for their choices, but never notice their needs, their dissatisfaction? How did we get so arrogant?

Apparent kingdom-dwellers are in conflict, roaring with pain and betrayal, struggling to know what is right and what is wrong, clashing, crushing... Some may seem strident and inflexible, but what caused that? We come back to motivation. They could be concerned about important things; we would do well to listen to them. Alternatively, defensiveness can come from fear and uncertainty. Others may seem a bit wishy-washy, too muddled to be kingdom-dwellers. We're not sure they tick all the boxes.

A culture of suspicion grows up between those who are the very ones entrusted with the kingdom message.

Where is the kingdom, now?

The kingdom has never been pinned down. Perhaps that's a good thing. Jesus didn't provide a 'step-by-step' guide; he used metaphor. The elusive reign of God is not always recognised, because we're looking through our old glasses and our short-term views. The kingdom of God is still near, but perhaps it's shedding some of the trappings we have pegged on it.

Institutions might testify to the reign of God but the reign itself is not a human institution. It cannot be confined inside walls of our making nor held within our carefully-worded definitions.

We cannot catalogue the kingdom of God.

Visions of kingdom

When our visions of kingdom seem to clash with those of other kingdom seekers, we need to seek harder. This might be a lifetime's journey. There may be no quick fixes. There may be a lifetime of disagreement, but we pray we will still seek, still love, still embody God's grace.

Whatever our weakness, God is stronger. Whatever our foolishness, God is still wiser. Maybe cracks are needed for the light to creep in – or out – again. Maybe shattering comes before mending. Maybe, amid all the noise, we aren't hearing the whispers that take place outside of the public sphere. Maybe we all need to get off our soap boxes and start loving each other – yes even when we are supremely unlovable, insufferable, inflexible, wishy-washy or messy.

What if we stripped it down and just came to seek God together, consistently and constantly? You and me, together, with all of our differences? If we believe in this God, if we both claim truth, it should be a delight, not a threat, to direct our puzzlement to the One we both worship. Let's come to God, saying together, *your kingdom come.*

Somewhere, right now, two people with two different viewpoints are praying together, in the name of Jesus, under the banner of love.

Such is the kingdom.

O God, acknowledging you as king
means a reshaping of my life,
a loyalty to you alone and to your ways.
Help me seek your kingdom here
and look forward to the day when
your reign is seen in everything.

REFLECT

- What do you think about when somebody mentions the 'kingdom of God'?
- How does the idea of God's reign affect how you live now?
- What would it mean to have this as your life's priority?

He came to that which was his own,
but his own did not receive him.
Yet to all who did receive him,
to those who believed in his name,
he gave the right to become children of God –
children born not of natural descent,
nor of human decision or a husband's will,
but born of God.
John 1:11-13 (NIV)

Chapter 17
Compelled by love

We know love by this, that he laid down his life for us –
and we ought to lay down our lives for one another.
1 John 3:16

What is love? It's a word often used, in different ways.

I love marzipan. I love the sea. I love my guinea pigs. I love my friends and family. I love my husband. I love God. I don't mean exactly the same with every one of those statements, although some are more related than others.

But love is at the heart of our story. We've seen how God's actions towards us are motivated by love; Jesus living and dying and living again are underpinned by extraordinary *love*.

Unfailing love
What kind of love does Jesus demonstrate? We witness it in his taking on flesh, living among us and as one of us, suffering with us and dying for us.

God in Jesus was 'us-focused'. This was God's great mission to humankind, kicking off the new covenant in a style that was not what anyone expected.

What does this kind of love look like? We could do worse than refer to 1 Corinthians 13 for inspiration, although we might want to put aside our associations of it as the 'wedding passage'! The original context is quite different. It comes in the middle of a section discussing the use of spiritual gifts. These gifts are good, says Paul, but without love, they are worthless. Tongues become 'a noisy gong'. Prophecy so potent as to understand all mysteries, faith that can move entire mountains – these, too, are nothing compared to love. Our best deeds, even giving up everything – our possessions, our bodies – so that we 'may boast', if done without love, gain us nothing at all. Without love as the motivator, the actions lose their meaning – *even if* they seem on the surface to be impressive and praiseworthy (vv.1-3).

Motives matter. The famous description of love that follows is given to a divided and somewhat competitive congregation, whom Paul has already reminded that 'there are many members and yet one body' (1 Corinthians 12:20). Now, he tells them that love is central to all that they do, in every way that they exercise their varied gifts. Using these gifts in unloving ways destroys their value.

Love underpins all; love gives *meaning*.

Our attempts at loving can seem flimsy. We often make love all about 'feelings'. That's not to say feelings are unimportant or unrelated to love. Feelings can be part of loving – there are those whom I see and, on seeing, am slammed by a rush of affection, delight and relief at their presence – 'felt love', if you like. But feelings are not the backbone of love.

The characteristics of love listed in 1 Corinthians 13 are primarily about attitude and action. Love is patient, kind, rejoices in truth, believes and hopes and endures all things. It's *not* envious, boastful, arrogant, rude, irritable, or insistent on its own way. It does *not* celebrate wrongdoing.

This unending love is made of something strong, something fierce, something determined. It shapes our spiritual practice and is a primary motivator of a Jesus follower. It unites our hearts.

We are so ready to make love what *we* want it to be, to share or, indeed, withhold it as we choose, to condemn others for being unloving, in very unloving ways! (I'm sorry, did I hit you with the plank in my eye?) In an age of soundbites, it's easy to pronounce judgments on the actions and motives of others, without recognising that which is present – or lacking – in ourselves.

The nature of Christ's love for us is demonstrated in a costly act of grace, that of laying down a life.

Sometimes we think of love as a 'snuggly' thing. To receive love can, indeed, be a comfort to us. But to *do* the loving, in a Jesus-like way? That is much harder.

Family likeness

Paul is not the only biblical writer to attempt to describe love. We read in 1 John that God *is* love (4:16). Because love is characteristic of God, it should be characteristic of God's children. John pulls no punches. 'Whoever does not love abides in death,' he says (1 John 3:14b). For John, love is a sign of who we are and of who we have become in Jesus.

We sense mystification in John's question: 'How does God's love abide in anyone who has the world's goods and sees a brother or sister in need and yet refuses help?' (3:17) Love is expressed in action.

For all our sermons, books, dialogues and songs, we still have a lot to learn about love.

Those who 'hate' brothers or sisters, whom they have seen, cannot love the God they have not seen (4:20). If we don't love each other, then a question mark hangs over our identity as the children of God. *We're not displaying the family likeness.* This is a challenge for us as church – how do we treat each other? The vitriol shown by some Christians towards one another – whichever side of whatever debate they are on – should concern us deeply. The cycle continues when we judge the 'other' for this behaviour and forget to examine our own.

Love does not mean we never say hard things, but it flavours them with patience and kindness. It resists cruelty; it doesn't snarl or bite. It's not rude or arrogant. This can be a particular challenge when we are consumed with a sense of rightness in our soundbite age. Sarcasm is all the rage. Do we speak condescendingly, dismissively? That is not love.

Can we love, even when others aren't acting with love towards *us*? This is grace. True grace is strong indeed. We get enthused about 'calling out' people on their behaviour – and rightly so, sometimes – but let's not forget to be responsible for our *own* behaviour. Let's remember grace in our responses to those who make barbed retorts and sweeping, unfair statements. We may think they don't deserve such a response, but this is grace, after all!

Knowing Jesus

> No one has ever seen God,
> it is God the only Son,
> who is close to the Father's heart,
> who has made him known.
>
> John 1:18

Love is a calling. It's to be pursued and perfected; it's not automatic. Sometimes it comes easy, when accompanied by feelings of affection and attachment. At other times, it's harder. Love is a primary characteristic of God, so we look to God to see what love is like. How do we look to God, who cannot be seen? Through Jesus.

Paul considers everything as loss compared to knowing Christ. All the old things he took pride in don't matter. They're just a stinky pile of rubbish in comparison. Knowing Christ is its own reward. To know Christ is to know God. This is the New Testament witness, for Christ is the one in whom we see the Father; the one in whom all the fulness of God dwells; the 'reflection of God's glory and the exact imprint of God's very being' and the Word, who is God.[67]

It is through Jesus we see God – a lens worth looking through, casting aside all other pairs of glasses, muddled mindsets, damaged core beliefs, self-driven world views.

The prism of Christ's love

For the love of Christ controls and compels us, because we have concluded this, that One died for all, therefore all died; and He died for all, so that all those who live would no longer live for themselves, but for Him who died and was raised for their sake.

2 Corinthians 5:14 -15 (AMP 1987)

Ever since I first read 2 Corinthians 5, I've wondered what it would mean to be compelled by the love of Christ, above all else, in my life. How would my life look, if it was motivated only by this love, pushing out the flimsy, foolish desires and the selfish motives I too often entertain?

The Greek word sometimes translated as 'compel' holds various shades of meaning. Where it's found in the New Testament, occurrences are interpreted according to context. It can mean to hold together, hem in, press on, restrict, impel... In this verse, we find that translations differ – as well as 'compel' (such as the NIV; the NRSV uses a similar 'urge us on'), we find 'control' and 'constrain', among others. The Amplified Bible, as quoted above, finds itself in the comfortable position of being able to use both 'control' *and* 'compel'!

In some ways, 'compel' and 'control' seem like opposites. Perhaps we might see it in terms of a finely focused motivation – urged on but also constrained by the love of Christ, avoiding selfish motives or things to boast about. There's no room for selfishness in the light of Christ's compelling and constraining love.

My eyes have trouble co-operating. I wear glasses for short-sightedness, but the real problem is my – wait for it – *decompensating esophoria*. My eyes drift inwards. My brain can't blend the two signals without the aid of prisms, which are put into the lenses of my glasses. Without them, I would have constant double vision.

I can just about manage to see in single vision without my

---

[67] See Philippians 3:7-9; John 14:9; Colossians 1:19; Hebrews 1:3; John 1:1

glasses at a very close distance, although these days even that results in a mild 'tugging' sensation. When the condition worsens, the warning signs include this 'tugging' in my eyes, which then start to ache from the strain of focusing. Eventually I experience a sliding in and out of single and double vision. The focus splits into two; it takes conscious effort to bring it back. When this becomes chronic, I'm prescribed more prisms in my glasses.

I wonder if to be compelled and constrained by Christ's love may be a little like a corrective prism, turning double vision into one united focus.

We have conflicting motives, many things that 'tug' at our spiritual eyes, causing them to slide. Our split vision – our divided hearts, our double-mindedness – can be brought together through the prism of Christ's love, training our gaze on him alone. The love of Christ enables us to resist the tugging of other desires.

Sharing Jesus

The gospel is a kingdom invitation, a call to 'come in', both generous and just. It calls us in and invites us to change our perspective, to reframe our world, to have our lives transformed.

We're called to share the love we have received, to pass on the invitation. How often have we downgraded love as a motivator for sharing the good news, because we have downgraded love itself, or made our own poor imitation of it?

Love is demonstrated by obedience to its source – God. We share the gospel because God calls us to do so. It is an obedience that springs out of love. If we base our intentions on results (which we cannot always see), we can lose heart. We end up being motivated by fear, but John tells us it is love that gives us boldness in the face of judgement, and that 'perfect love casts out fear' (1 John:17-18).

Do we worry too much about perceived 'results'? Does this stifle us, or, conversely, promote a kind of self-reliance? Either we end up doing nothing at all, or we rely so much on our own efforts it can seem that God has little to do with it. But this is a God whose strength is shown through weakness, whose wisdom is known via fools.[68]

If we are living to love others the way Christ loves us, we're not constantly looking for results. The motivator matters. Without it, we fall back on those same-old stories of wanting human

[68] See 1 Corinthians 1:27; 2 Corinthians 12:9

approval, clocking up points, ticking off lists, trying to measure the immeasurable.

Some people get nervous about the idea of 'evangelism', because they worry about themselves, their own abilities, and their results – or lack of them. I know, I've felt this myself. Others have shared their sense of inadequacy and worry with me, too.

I wonder – is results-based evangelism good? A straight yes/no might not be the most helpful answer. It *is* valuable to see what is effective in reaching out to people, in showing them the nature of the kingdom. It *is* useful to ask questions about why we do things in certain ways (because we've always done them? Or because they are the 'new thing' going around?).

Tools can be useful; there are helpful ways of doing and saying things, just as there are unhelpful ways. However, if the core motivation is anything less than the love of Christ, we will struggle. Have we forgotten that core? Our witness and our discipleship cannot go deep without this love underpinning it. Otherwise we rely on our own strength and confidence and, for some of us, this feels small indeed.

Rather than getting tangled up with 'success' and 'failure', perhaps we should just get on with loving, while acknowledging that in our humanity we will get it wrong sometimes, that our love is not perfected yet. God will work through our weaknesses; in fact, God specialises in such endeavours.

To be compelled by the love of Christ is a motivator that rises above rejection. For Jesus was rejected, insulted, dismissed, 'devalued' by the world, discouraged, denied and even betrayed by his friends, questioned, misunderstood, beaten, killed.

Scandalous love
'Everything that the Father gives me will come to me,
and anyone who comes to me I will never drive away...'

John 6:37

Christ bears our wounds.

Remember that, next time you find yourself bleeding. He's right there with you. It's not easy; it doesn't work as a platitude *because* it isn't easy. People can say these things to 'make us feel better'. It may not make you feel better; *you don't have to feel it should.* But Christ bleeds with you, regardless. The one who experienced ultimate rejection offers us permanent acceptance.

As Word made flesh, Jesus showed love in welcoming the

unwelcomed, befriending the friendless, seeing past stereotypes and challenging other people's judgements. In his death, Jesus demonstrated love at its bleakest and most powerful, made more so because of who Jesus was, because of the divine initiative behind this new covenant. In his resurrection, death itself was overturned. This extraordinary love was opened up to us all.

We are still called to follow, after the passing of two millennia; we still stagger to the cross and are scandalised by love such as this. We still argue with it, aghast at such sacrifice; we still weep at it, when we comprehend its purpose. We still gawp at the empty tomb, perplexed and afraid; we still fall on our knees as we encounter the risen Christ. We are still given the Spirit of life and find this ancient love planted new in our hearts.

The love of Christ compels us; it is this love we pursue, this love that endures over the ages. This love we reject at our peril, when we make a mockery of it through our actions and inaction.

This love, this terrifying and consoling love – God's love, for us.

Tell me again what love is, Lord.
Tell me your marvellous story.
Remind me of your nail-pierced hands;
hold me against your wounded side.
Show me again what love is, Lord.

REFLECT
- How have you experienced the love of Christ?
- How do think love has been understood – or misunderstood?
- When do you find it hard to love others?

Blessed be the God and Father of our Lord Jesus Christ who[...] destined us for adoption as his children through Jesus Christ, according to the good pleasure of his will, to the praise of his glorious grace that he freely bestowed on us in the Beloved.

... In Christ we have also obtained an inheritance, having been destined according to the purpose of him who accomplishes all things according to his counsel and will, so that we, who were the first to set our hope on Christ, might live for the praise of his glory. In him you also, when you had heard the word of truth, the gospel of your salvation, and had believed in him, were marked with the seal of the promised Holy Spirit; this is the pledge of our inheritance towards redemption as God's own people, to the praise of his glory.

Ephesians 1:3,5,6; 11-14

Chapter 18
Led by the Spirit

'... see, I am sending upon you what my Father promised;
so stay here in the city until you have been clothed with
power from on high.'
Luke 24:49

The story of Jesus has astonishing power. But it's not enough. To be disciples of Jesus, to be compelled by the love of Jesus, requires the *presence* of Jesus with us.

When Jesus returned to heaven, what then? 'Wait,' he told his disciples. 'Wait until you have been clothed with power from on high.'

However much Jesus had inspired them by his life and instructed them through his teachings, his followers needed a divine equipping. This was the same equipping Jesus himself received at his baptism.

The gifting of the Holy Spirit to God's people was the next chapter of this new covenant reality. The Holy Spirit of God, the divine breath, anointed the disciples of Jesus with holy fire, urging or nudging them this way and that, gifting them for every purpose, strengthening them for every journey, reminding them of Jesus' words, *being Christ in them.*

Breath of life
In the beginning when God created the heavens and the earth,
the earth was a formless void and darkness covered the face
of the deep, while a wind from God swept over the face of the
waters.

Genesis 1:1-2

The Spirit of God gives life. The Spirit renews, restores, refreshes, enlivens. God interacts with the creation by the Spirit, but the Spirit is not an impersonal force. The Spirit is distinct, unpredictable.

The Spirit cannot be boxed.

The Spirit has inspired craftsmen, prophets and kings. At Pentecost, the Spirit filled the gathered disciples, astonishing those around them and bringing more people into this new community. The Spirit equips the church for living as followers of Jesus, enabling us to live in kingdom ways. Together we share in the Spirit.[69] The Spirit enables us to glorify God in our worship and helps us in our prayers. As the Body of Christ, we are also given specific and diverse gifts by this Spirit, drawing us deeper into our experience of God and reflecting Jesus to our world.

The Spirit generates life and *regenerates*, giving new life; the Spirit is agent of creation and *recreation*.

We grieve the Spirit when we sin; the Spirit tells us when our hearts are moving away from God. The Spirit reveals truth to us. The Spirit inspires our reading of scripture (the same Spirit who inspired the writing of them).

The Spirit works with us, whispering hope and wisdom, occasionally overwhelming us, often challenging and convicting us.

The Spirit motivates us and equips us to live the life to which we are called.

God's children

> For those who are led by the Spirit of God are the children of God. The Spirit you received does not make you slaves, so that you live in fear again; rather, the Spirit you received brought about your adoption to sonship. And by him we cry, 'Abba, Father.' The Spirit himself testifies with our spirit that we are God's children. Now if we are children, then we are heirs – heirs of God and co-heirs with Christ, if indeed we share in his sufferings in order that we may also share in his glory.
>
> Romans 8:14-17 (NIV)

The Spirit brings about our adoption, identifying us as God's children. We are freed from slavery and released into family. Readers of Paul's letter to the Romans would have known that certain privileges were conferred with adoption. The word 'sonship' implies a privileged position – we are not only children, we are *heirs*. The Spirit is the seal and pledge of our inheritance.[70]

To be adopted as God's children and to be led by the Spirit means that our attitudes, our conduct, become God-pleasing

---

[69] See Philippians 2:1
[70] See Ephesians 1:13-14

and God-revealing. We don't have to feel that our traits, our past experiences – those old default settings – are our masters.

What Paul often refers to as the 'flesh' has these powerful drivers, including lust, greed and other destructive behaviours. This flesh is not body-only specific, as it bears fruit in our attitudes – in our minds – as well. Paul compares a flesh-driven life to one led by the Spirit.[71]

Our lives, led by the Spirit, testify to who we now are in Christ.

'Flesh' and 'spirit' are not abstract versus concrete (as they were for Plato). To be ruled by the flesh is just as powerful with abstract ideologies as it is with bodily appetites. Likewise to be led by the Spirit is transformative at all levels. Our whole being – physical, mental, emotional – is attuned to the character of Christ.

The flesh means death – and all that is dead in us.

The Spirit brings *life.*

The old and the new

However, the flesh can still exercise a hold on us. There are whispers in our lives. These whispers repeat old lies, tell us we can never change, poke and prod at our faith, make our heads turn this way and that instead of looking forward. We live among the whispers, and sometimes we listen so much that they become shouts, drowning out what we have learned, stealing our joy, making us careless or defensive.

In our attempts to control them we can fall into old traps of legalism, denouncing others who have more nuanced viewpoints. Instead of freedom, we embrace dogmatism. We talk big and we talk righteous but on the inside, things are muddier than we'd care to admit. Only when we admit this mess can we start taking steps to change it, and invite the Spirit to transform us once again.

Are we prepared for the Spirit to lead us, to let go of the stuff that prevents us from living as Jesus followers?

We easily re-adopt old habits, reattach to our corrupted defaults, forgetting that we have a new template now and that this new reality brings with it abundance, if we would open our eyes and not start getting bogged down by 'the flesh' again.

Following the groove

Think of a ball rolling down a groove. The groove guides the ball but, tracing it back, we discover that the *ball created the groove.* Every

[71] e.g. in Galatians 5

time it rolled that way, the groove became more pronounced. The ball rolls more easily down the groove it has created. It takes more effort to send it a different way. Every roll deepens the groove.

When we repeat behaviour, it becomes a standard progression. Our brains develop synaptic pathways which are strengthened with each 'repeat'. The more we do something, the more natural it becomes to do it. We respond that way to criticism because it's what we have always done. We walk that way because we always have. In the end, it feels the most natural thing in the world. We forget to think of it as negative, and if we do, we shrug, lower our faces, and say 'it's just the way I am. I can't change.' Change in the face of this well-worn path feels impossible.

We can establish 'new grooves' but it takes effort and practice. Once a habit is made, it's easier to slip back to it, more so than if it had never existed. There will always be a tendency to go that way.

We can try to prevent such grooves forming – trying to nurture wisdom and self-awareness, alert to temptation and the things 'of the flesh'. But inevitably we all make mistakes and fall into negative behaviour patterns. These become our battlegrounds; our acknowledged weaknesses. We need help to get and keep free of them.

To be led by the Spirit and not the flesh is about a whole new groove, a new pattern for us to follow. Just as our core beliefs are challenged and cracked open, our patterns of behaviour are also shaken by the Spirit reality. We are not be 'slaves to sin' anymore. Our only master is Jesus – and it is the Spirit who makes Jesus present in our lives.

A new kind of normal

Have you ever stayed in a hotel room and discovered the bath or shower was rather less clean than you would like? You notice every speck, every hair (ugh). You don't know where it came from, it's not from you. It's distasteful. But what if you walked into your bathroom at home and looked at it from the same perspective?[72]

Our less desirable habits can become so much part of the

---

[72] If your bathroom is *always* sparkling clean in every nook and cranny, even down behind the loo where the pipe meets the wall, this analogy may not work for you.

scenery that we barely notice them. If we do, we can quickly move into the next room and forget about them. Sometimes you need the glare of sunshine to see the dust covering everything. We aren't always aware of the habits we've acquired or the situations we're in; there's not enough light to see them. Our hearts are so dingy we don't notice the grime that prevents us from shining.

Our motivators become part of the furniture; we hardly see them. Our ways of thinking feel so normal that we don't notice anything untoward. It seems strange to be asked to think or act differently. But the transforming gospel of Christ is not one just to paint the surface; it expands into the deepest crevices of our lives. If we sign on half-heartedly, we miss out on that infilling, that total transformation. In fact, we can't sign on half-heartedly because it makes a nonsense of it. The gospel cannot take root in such shallow ground; it withers and dies.

> *Have you attempted to paint the surface of your*
> *heart in gospel colours,*
> *but at your core, not really changed?*

What grooves are we forming? What trenches do we get ourselves into? We are called out of old behaviours and challenged to listen and be led by the Spirit, through whom we bear fruit. A Spirit-led life is evidenced by the fruit we bear in our whole lives. We don't produce this fruit alone. Instead, it is God working in us and through us. There is no place for self-reliance. If we rely on our own efforts we will fail. Only God's Holy Spirit can lift us from the mire, only God in Christ can save us from our sinfulness. And in Christ we find not just help but grace – so that when we slip up, as we all do, we know that we can start again with the Spirit leading us.

The life led by the Spirit is one that requires a new inclination, because 'the flesh' was put to death in Jesus' dying for us. The Spirit gives us a new template for living. We need to tune into the Spirit's leading, to seek the Spirit's empowering, to sense the new and beautiful paths we are called to follow, and not get stuck back in our old grooves again. Because, let's be honest, we need *continual* transformation in our lives. Other things and desires will try to pull us off track.

Every day is a refresher course in living by the Spirit.

Holy equipping

... where the Spirit of the Lord is, there is freedom.

2 Corinthians 3:17

The guide of God's people is no longer the Old Covenant Law, 'engraved in letters of stone' (2 Corinthians 3:7). Instead it is the Spirit, who directs us on the path to holiness. The Spirit breaks chains and old mindsets, sealing us to Christ and writing God's law on our hearts.

This Spirit can create within us a desire to please God and know God better, a desire to follow and to imitate Jesus, who embodied a Spirit-led humanity. We imitate Jesus by keeping in step with the Spirit, being filled with the Spirit, being led by the Spirit. We need to be sensitive to what the Spirit is saying to us, reminding us, calling us to be. The Spirit is the one who *enables* us to be disciples, to live under God's reign. We are entrusted with a mission, but this is not God 'relying' on us – rather, it is a call for us to rely on God and on God's Spirit equipping us.

The call to pursue God is not a passive thing, but reacts to the love and grace we have been shown. It's not done in our own strength, but by the Spirit's power. Lukewarm following is not going to be enough. It's not going to see me through. It's not going to inspire me or help me in my life. I should know that by now, but it's so easy to slip into it, my focus dividing in so many ways, my motives getting more and more muddled.

The Spirit helps me pray when I have no words, searches me to my depths and likewise reveals to me a taster of the depths of God.[73] The Spirit reminds me of my true motivation and helps to unite my heart in praise of the One I follow. When my motives are confused, I look to the Spirit to shake them up and shake them out. When I struggle to find meaning in my life, I rely on the Spirit to open my eyes again and restore my sense of purpose.

This is the Spirit of God, the Spirit of glory. Do we downplay the fierce beauty of this divine flame, this life-altering breath? Do we neglect to surrender to the Spirit of holiness, prioritising instead our fleshly desires, or our own attempts at managing these desires?

It is the Holy Spirit who makes Christ's love real to us today. Through the Holy Spirit, we know Jesus and therefore the Father; the triune God is made real in our lives.

If we choose to align ourselves with the Spirit, that Spirit will

[73] Romans 8:26-27

shape us and propel us into both the ordinary and the extraordinary, creating within us a seal which smacks of God's glory, light which diminishes darkness.

> *She speaks.*
> *Can you hear her?*
> *The dove of God,*
> *her whisper, compelling;*
> *the wild goose*
> *clamouring and crying;*
> *the fire burning and refining;*
> *the wind stirring and shifting –*
> *invisible breath filling you,*
> *empowering you,*
> *enabling you*
> *to be something better,*
> *something purer*
> *and kinder...*
> *Something more marvellous*
> *than you ever thought you could be.*
> *Her touch, moulding,*
> *forming life again,*
> *birthing new beginnings,*
> *destroying the ugliness within.*

In the Old Testament scriptures, the Spirit was only 'bestowed' on those with a specific role or a special purpose. At Pentecost, Peter proclaimed a new era, in which the words of the ancient prophet, Joel, are fulfilled (Acts 2:14-21). God was pouring out his Spirit on all people – young and old, male and female. In this act, old divisions lost their relevance.

The Spirit-filled believers were to be known by the name of Jesus.

REFLECT
- What role does the Holy Spirit play in defining who you are?
- What 'grooves' of behaviour do you see in your life?
- In what way do you need to re-tune to the Spirit's leading?

Before the coming of this faith we were held in
custody under the law,
locked up until the faith that was to come would be revealed.
So the law was our guardian until Christ came that
we might be justified by faith.
Now that this faith has come, we are no longer under a guardian.
So in Christ Jesus you are all children of God through faith,
for all of you who were baptised into Christ have clothed yourselves
with Christ.
Galatians 3:23-27 (NIV)

Chapter 19

Above every name

Therefore God also highly exalted him
and gave him the name
that is above every name,
so that at the name of Jesus
every knee should bend,
in heaven and on earth and under the earth,
and every tongue should confess
that Jesus Christ is Lord,
to the glory of God the Father.
Philippians 2:9-11

In a changeable world, where roots don't always go as deep as we would like, when life pulls us about, we look for a definition to which we can cling. We look for a sense of meaning.

There are so many things, so many definers in our lives, so many labels – those which stick to us no matter how hard we try to get rid of them, those which never stick, even though we desperately try to make them adhere to us because we want to fit in for whatever reason.

But only one Name matters.

A new covenant world

There is no longer Jew or Greek, there is no longer slave or free,
there is no longer male and female; for all of you are one in
Christ Jesus. And if you belong to Christ, then you are Abraham's
offspring, heirs according to the promise.

Galatians 3:28-29

Under the banner of Christ, other divisions and labels fade in importance. Paul reflects on this in relation to the separate groups who were coming together in the new Christian faith, springing from Judaism but refocusing around this person they called Jesus, the messiah. *You are all one in the messiah.*

The Jews had been waiting for the messiah. The non-Jews, the Gentiles, did not have this experience of waiting in the same focused way; they did not have the same expectations of what a messiah would be. However, that's not to say they didn't have assumptions about the divine and what characterised someone favoured or chosen by a god.

It was a climate of belief, of many beliefs, jangling round. The cross of Christ was foolishness to the Gentiles and a stumbling block to the Jews – a struggle and/or scandal to both groups, one seeking signs, the other seeking wisdom.[74] But it was the cross of Christ that now brought them together. A new wisdom, a new way of seeing, was required from all of them, and they had to leave behind their preconceptions and be bold in exploring what God had in store for them.

Together, they were *named*, all of them, 'in Christ'. In Christ, they were neither Jew nor Gentile. There was neither slave nor free. There was no male and female. These 'labels' may have denoted something about them and their circumstances, but they were not what mattered most. They needed no longer to divide them, because of the unifying act of Christ. It wouldn't be easy. It would get messy, and still does, as we try to work out how to be together in Christ despite our differences, our backgrounds, our previous assumptions.

Paul's letters touch on this messy reality, as different people have differing points of view as to how things should be done in a 'new covenant world'. His letter to the Galatians is a howl against stipulations that they need to meet the demands of the Law (especially circumcision) to be part of the Christian community. That is not your identifier, Paul says. Your identifier is that you are in Christ.

Our identifier is to be in Christ. It is not the Law, which Christ both fulfilled and superseded. The Law was the guardian, the custodian until Jesus came, the great sacrifice made, the resurrection reality dawned upon us. Those of us who have never been under the Law are now joined with those that were guided by it.

Those who were not God's people are made God's people through Christ. This is our primary definition; this is the meaning of our lives, *this* is who we are.

In Christ

Every identifier, 'label' and 'box' is nothing compared to the vast, inclusive reality of being 'in Christ'. There should be no part of our

[74] See 1 Corinthians 1:22-24

lives divorced from this identity. It informs every aspect of our lives. Each moment of each day, whomever we are with, whatever we are doing, we are 'in Christ'.

Christianity is not just for Sundays. Our 'gathering moments' are important (whenever they are). We are in Christ *together* and it's good to regularly remind ourselves of this. They inspire us, encourage us and motivate us. However, we don't leave our Christ-identity behind when we exit a room or move into a different group of people. Whether we are walking down a path in a forest, staring at a screen, dancing, sleeping or lying awake wishing for sleep to come, we are still together in Christ. Every breath is part of our unity with and in Christ. Trying to shunt our identity in Christ into just another box does no good to us – it can even do harm, because it means we have divided something that should never be divided, something that is whole, something that supersedes the rest.

If we are indeed in Christ, then we demonstrate Christ-ness to others. We become windows to the fullness of God's love, mini-perspectives on a great reality. These are limited – we are flawed human beings, after all – but our small testimonies form part of a marvellous mosaic. A mosaic which witnesses to a *person*, not an institution or a system.

The church is the body of Christ. This body is comprised of those who are 'in Christ'. We are held together in all our diversity, by the person of Jesus. We would do well to remind ourselves of the profound simplicity of this when we get weighed down with structures and methods – which can be useful or awkward, good or bad. These things are not the core truth of our identity. We need to challenge ourselves when we begin to take pride in our 'category' of Christianity. Just as all other labels lose their stickiness when we embrace the Name above every name, the church in all its different expressions is held in this one primary identity – this one person.

This Jesus.

Called to diverse unity

Christians can be as prone to labelling as anyone else. We get so attached to a label that we act as if it were a salvation necessity. We have bound up so much in that label, whether it's to do with denominational preference, or whether we're 'evangelical', 'liberal', something else or a subsection of something else – terms that mean different things depending on our geographical location, personal context or worldview, which only exacerbates misunderstanding.

We start proclaiming different kinds of Jesus, making our interpretation the only one. (Are you thinking of someone else – an individual or a group – as you read this? You may have good reasons for doing so, but are you brave enough to look first at yourself?)

In clinging to our various labels (and our equally varied understandings of them), we can create unnecessary 'dividers'. The labels themselves may not be bad, just ways of identifying difference and preference. In a diverse world, with many parts, labels can be useful.

But in comparison to being named 'in Christ', they are of little value. Remember, Paul declared all his impressive labels to be rubbish in comparison to knowing Jesus. It's not about the lack of importance of one label, but acknowledging the astounding value of another, which eclipses all else.

This is why under the name of Christ so many diverse people are joined. It's a call to unity. This naming gives us our value and our primary identity. Meaning and motivation – at a profound level – are found here.

When we look away from that 'uniting name' and hitch our loyalties to other, lesser categories, we begin to bicker amongst ourselves. It becomes about comparison, rank and position. We divide along lines of opinion, interpretation and preference. We get confused over certain issues, worry about what we should think or believe, and 'bite and devour one another' in ways that are most un-Christ like.[75]

So what do we do when we disagree?

It's important to recognise motivation. If both parties' motives are to honour Christ, this is good but, because we 'see dimly', it doesn't mean we necessarily agree! However, if we recognise that motivation within each other, we at least have a chance of disagreeing graciously and conversing gently, even prayerfully.

It may still be extremely exasperating(!), but we can recognise Christ in one another, even in disagreement. Unfortunately, we can dig so deep into our own understanding that we fail to see Christ in our opponent – and if we are seeing them as an opponent, that's a problem in itself. One person may try to reconcile and the other refuse; this is painful. Or both may be at loggerheads, clinging to their own 'badges' and all too ready to fling more labels at each other.

We get so busy defending our beliefs about God that we neglect

[75] See Galatians 5:15

to seek God. Before we know it, we are entrenched in human battles and God's kingdom-reality is nowhere to be seen in either of us. We get in the way of the very gospel we are preaching.

In our flawed humanity, sometimes we do not reach the best of situations; we end up having to accept the 'least worst', the best of bad options. This is hard, but it can mean a separation of sorts for each one's spiritual health. Even Paul and Barnabas had a sharp falling out and parted ways because of it.[76]

Held in Christ, the flagship of grace, there are many opinions and interpretations. There may be those differences we consider 'inessential', but also those that feel more serious. We think of them as 'deal-breakers'; the places we cannot go; the compromises we cannot allow. We may well be right. We might also be wrong. In the end, only the Name we claim, only the One we follow, can fully perceive our motives, our rightness and our wrongness. At times of stalemate, we can only commit them to him.

Final judgement is not our call.

Spiritual superiority

There are many things to which I don't have an answer. Many issues where my response would please neither 'side' of a debate! Life is multi-shaded and I confess I cannot always detect the right 'hue'. But those claiming to be kingdom-seekers, do indeed need to start with seeking – praying, asking, chasing God, longing for God's Spirit.

We express ourselves differently. We vary in personality, in our likes and in our dislikes – including in our ways of expressing worship to God. This reflects our diversity and enables us to learn about God in many ways. Problems occur when we claim that our way is better or more 'spiritual', looking down on those who practise their faith differently. They may feel the same about us; we spend all our time staring down our noses at each other! We don't understand that way of doing things; we don't identify with it – we don't see how anyone else could.

We create add-ons to faith – extra hoops, further requirements in order not just to be Christian but a 'real' Christian. We dub each other 'immature' or 'naïve', 'rigid' or 'patronising'.

We declare the lordship of Christ and believe in his resurrection,[77] but when we make it about lesser things, we look away from the One who gives us – all of us – our identity.

[76] See Acts 15:36-41
[77] See Romans 10:9

We create our own entry requirements for the kingdom of God. We are right to wince at the idea of this – for this is what Jesus accused some of the Pharisees of doing – shutting people out of the kingdom.

When we look upon someone and use phrases (out loud or in our heads) such as 'too much of this' or 'not enough of that'; when we make a habit of criticising other peoples' journeys of faith, we are in murky waters.

What motivates us to make such claims, such criticisms? We might 'mean well', so enthusiastic are we about our own point of view – but the reality is that if we begin to judge others on lesser labels, instead of embracing each other in Christ, we lose the most essential thing of all. For in Christ we find the meaning of who we are and who we are all called to be.

Praying in the Name

We pray in Jesus' name.

Prayer is essential for unity, for our life 'in Christ'. Prayer focuses our hearts on God's will, not our own (although we need to be wary of making our prayers a summary of our own agendas, or quests for human approval).

When we pray 'in Jesus' name', we bear witness that it is Jesus who motivates and defines us, that it is Jesus who is our primary purpose; that all our disparate identifiers are superseded by this; that the prayers we pray honour Jesus' life and God's will for us.

When we pray in Jesus' name, we recognise that it is through Jesus that we can approach God in prayer with confidence, that in him we can cry *abba*, Father.

When we pray in Jesus' name, we surrender our needs, our opinions, our desires, our labels, all the drivers of our lives to Jesus. We declare our identity and recognise his authority. Our prayers come out of our relationship with Jesus and acknowledgement of Jesus as Lord. For at his name, every knee will bow.[78]

This is not a name to be taken lightly. Do your prayers honour Jesus, reflecting your identity in him?

In Jesus' name, we pray. We can chant this like a formula – the bit before 'amen'. But the name we are invoking is the name above all other names, a name recognised by both angels and demons, a name that is binding, a name that has power, a healing name, a name that banishes darkness.

[78] See Philippians 2:10

It's not an answer to a crossword puzzle, not a ritual sentence to complete a prayer. It is the purpose and attitude behind all our prayers. It is the focus of our lives. We call on the name of Jesus, for in this name we are known by God. We cry this name as a summons to the One who saves us; it is the name that hovers on our lips and abides in our hearts at times of crisis and of blessing. Jesus – name above all names.

This name is more than the word 'Jesus', which has been a given name for others. *This* Jesus, this messiah – his 'name' is more than letters assembled in a certain order. This is Emmanuel – God with us, saviour, redeemer, servant, master, Lord, the lamb that was led to the slaughter, the Lion of Judah who roars. All these and more are held within this identity – this name above all other names.

A name above all names requires complete loyalty, for that name surpasses all others. We would do well to remember this, when we pray, when we speak, when we work together – and when we disagree.

For the One who is thus named in turn names us, declaring us sisters and brothers. Together, we are in Christ. Together, we are co-heirs with him. Together, we are the children of God.

Loving Lord,
teach me to honour your Name
and to find my identity in you.

REFLECT

- When have you judged someone else for their expression of faith?
- When has someone else judged yours?
- What do you think it means to be known by the Name above all names?

Batter my heart, three-person'd God; for you
As yet but knock; breathe, shine, and seek to mend;
That I may rise, and stand, o'erthrow me, and bend
Your force, to break, blow, burn, and make me new.
John Donne

Chapter 20

Unite my heart!

*I wait for the Lord, my soul waits
and in his word I put my hope.
My soul waits for the Lord,
more than watchmen wait for the morning,
more than watchmen wait for the morning.*
Psalm 130:5-6

How long has your heart been divided?

I have my suspicions that to unite a divided heart is a painful process. Misplaced loyalties need to be discarded – and we've formed lasting attachments to some of them. Some of our most tender desires may need to be sacrificed. A lot of things might need confessing to ourselves and to God – what it is we really want, and whether that is what we should be wanting, and how it all ties together under the great uniting name of Jesus.

To gather up the pieces of our fragmented lives and focus them on one profound longing, one primary motivator, is no small feat – especially if we are in disrepair, if we feel fractured beyond our ability to mend, if we are pulled this way and that, if we are ridden with labels good and bad.

I wonder how to do it – to unite my heart – as might you. As I grew in my Christian faith I would read a lot of 'spiritual' stuff. Things would be said about who I needed to be – things I wanted to be, but I kept wanting to ask: *how?*

The trouble is, the 'how' is not easy to pin down. It's like someone telling you that you need to forgive. *How?* Let go. *How?* Love. *How?* Believe. *How?* However much we may want to forgive, let go, love, these aren't things we know how to control or demand of ourselves.

Our hearts aren't comprised of dot-to-dot puzzles that can be traced with a bit of concentration and a cup of tea. We can't usually change our deepest feelings with the sheer force of our own efforts.

How do I challenge my inconsistencies? What do I do about

my doubt? It really is only God who knows. I hope that my seasons of seeking and my deep dark moments of longing for God count for something against the toxicity of the anxiety which too often drives me.

Change takes time, and cannot be achieved alone – not if that change is what I've been talking about – a heart united in pursuit of Jesus. It will not happen with one person exactly as it does for another. There is no one template, no one label, no one set of instructions as to how to deal with the human heart, how to navigate that fragile core.

We've already been shaped and driven in unique ways. In order for further shaping, the approach will be just as unique. Not in ways we would necessarily ask for, expect or anticipate. The journey might be far more meandering than we imagine; we spend longer in darkness than we think should be allowed; we are as much moulded by befuddlement as by revelation.

'Unite my heart' – the Psalmist's cry is a plea, not a statement of intent. This is a *prayer*, not a New Year's Resolution.

We cannot unite our own hearts towards God. It's not a spiritual accomplishment we can achieve. Our God has always been the one who stretches out to save us, interacts with us, woos us, confuses us, talks to us, keeps silence with us, works with us in our lives through the Spirit.

It's a co-operative act. We need to seek it; we need to be willing to change – to drop the unimportant. We need to listen to God's whisper or, if we are dulled or distracted, God's roar. We need to risk losing human approval, to sacrifice our desire to be liked and instead seek to love others with all that we have.

Sacrifice isn't a popular concept. Jesus on the cross scandalises us. We cannot always see the depth of the action, the life-shaking, world-changing, upturning grace that is at work among us.

Once when I was going through a particularly difficult time in my faith, I prayed: 'I want to know who you are... who you *really* are.' Implicit behind that question was 'and I don't care what that is'. Which may make some of you furrow your brows, because surely, we should care who God is? But that wasn't where I was coming from; that wasn't the question I was asking.

It was a fierce cry of following whatever it took. I had to let go of my assumptions, my own ideas of who God 'should' be. Even if what I discovered disturbed me or destabilised me, I wanted the truth, with all its tenderness and its terror, all its blinding light and paralysing darkness. I sought the God of light *and* dark. Whatever

I found, I offered my allegiance, such as it was. (These desperate, rather unorthodox pleas end up feeling like some of my most powerful prayers.)

I wonder, if I prayed every day to the God I claim to follow, worship and obey – *unite my heart* (whatever it may entail), what would happen? Do I dare to pray again in this way? Do I dare ask this of God, a God who, if I believe what I say I believe, is vaster than an entire universe of light and dark?

Our ideas about a creator of such a universe can only ever be *tame*. But God cannot be tamed.

Continuing the journey

Give me an undivided heart. Those words tugged at me from a young age; something in them awoke a longing within me. Perhaps because, as life moved on, I could feel myself disintegrate, get pulled in all directions. I became aware of the muddledness of my motives, of the times when that desire to follow was not as strong as it had been, or as strong as I wanted it to be.

Where does the journey end? Not here, although this is the final chapter of this book. What got me this far? What led *you* here?

I've longed to know God. When I haven't, I've gone rummaging, looking to reclaim that longing. At times I have gazed from afar and wished to be more than what I am, less inclined to that which tugs me away from the profound and the beautiful. Sometimes I've been sitting uncomfortably at the edge, not willing to throw myself into new possibilities; sometimes I've been straddling a tower and doubting the existence of a ledge. Sometimes I have claimed allegiance to something I cannot see and have not seen for such a long, long time.

Such is the call of faithfulness. Such is a heart trained on one goal, on one *person*. I build my life around that One. What, of that building, is enduring (and what is not) remains to be seen.

Life is a journey of valley and hill, of mountain-climbing and verge-sitting. I do a lot of verge-sitting. Sometimes I think God sits there with me. Sometimes God prods at me or calls me from afar. Sometimes I hear that call and raise my head. Sometimes I don't, too consumed with my own self and the small bits of rubble I have collected as if they were treasure. When I do this, the Spirit grieves.

Sometimes I feel that I have been sliding backwards and must start again. This isn't a repeat journey; I have to find another way. There are different treasures to be found – things I would not have noticed the first-time round – so much more precious than the rubble in my pockets. The Spirit sifts my heart, a painful process, upending my motives and showing me what measly ambitions I have fostered, what selfishness has taken root. It feels like backtracking, but perhaps it is growth, just a sort I haven't yet recognised.

Sometimes I need time to clear out the rubble, scrub at the dingy bits and allow God into the dimmer parts of my heart as well as the brighter. Only then can my heart be united.

I need to turn back to God in a continual repentance, a continual re-gauging of my life. Each day is a new beginning and a new chance; within it God is waiting to speak, if only I would listen.

So often I do not listen.

Awe

The fear of the Lord is the beginning of wisdom,
and knowledge of the Holy One is understanding.
Proverbs 9:10 (NIV)

My thoughts are drawn to the idea of the God who comes to us – as God has in the past, speaking through prophets and rescuing nations, ultimately in Jesus, Word-made-flesh; as God continues to do in our present age, through the pouring out and indwelling of the Spirit, expressed in love by the church; as God who will come – the pulling together of everything, when the curtain between heaven and earth is finally ripped asunder, when Christ is recognised by all as Lord, when God dwells with humanity in fullness of glory.

To ponder these things gives my heart focus – the drive to seek God's kingdom, to recognise God's activity in the now and the not yet, to yearn for God's Spirit at work in my life, to demonstrate Christ's love to those around me, to believe in more to come – a new creation, profound presence and reunion.

I come back to where I started.

To *awe.*

When we are in awe of something it takes all our focus; we are wrapped up in wonder. We may feel a little afraid, because what we are in awe of is so big. So important. So *bright.*

We can barely look at its brightness, but at the same time we cannot look away from it, it is all there is, it is the source of all wonder and truth and hope and holiness.

> *O God*
> *Founder of reality*
> *Judge of living and dead*
> *Lover of humanity*
> *Saviour of us all*
> *O God*
> *Majestic and tender*
> *Awesome and gentle*
> *You are*
> *You are*
>
> *You are.*

'Teach me your way, O Lord, and I will walk in your truth; Give me an undivided heart,' the Psalmist prays, 'that I may fear your name'. What does it mean to fear God's name? In awe and reverence, we recognise the God-ness of God. We long for knowledge of God and encounter with God. Our beliefs have an impact on how we live. 'I will praise you,' the prayer-song continues, 'O Lord my God, with all my heart; I will glorify your name for ever. For great is your love towards me; you have delivered me from the depths of the grave.'[79]

The psalmist celebrated escape from earthly death, now we celebrate something stronger, wider and even more amazing. Because of Jesus, we have 'passed from death to life' (John 5:24). The deeper reality of the life that is offered shines before us, if we would only stop staring at our shoes.

The struggle

Do we forget that we worship the God who comes to us? Do we get too consumed with our static view of reality? The compelling and constraining love of Christ is active. In our own lives, what counts is 'faith expressing itself through love' (Galatians 5:6, NIV). Love is an expression of belief as well as an act of compassion. The love of Christ is expressed in the cross, an act defended and vindicated by the resurrection, the crowning of the King who came and comes and is still to come.

When it all seems too much, I can only look to Jesus. For meaning and motivation, for faith and hope. For the ultimate demonstration of love.

We look to his coming. We train our hearts and minds to follow

[79] Psalm 86:11-13, NIV

his steps, we run after him because it is all we can do, despite the dust and the murk and the difficulties thrown at us. That is pursuit of God, that is a united heart, seeking to walk in God's truth and fear God's name, because God is both far beyond us and close beside us. The fierceness of God may make us quake; the love of God might cause us to tremble; the compassion of God can bring us to tears at the hardness of our own hearts.

An undivided heart is not a 'feeling'; it is not waking up one morning with a spiritual superiority complex; it is not thinking that we have 'made it' and really *are* 'holier than thou'. It does not mean we never struggle.

It *is* the struggle.

In our quest to know God better, we push on through the drudgery and doldrums of life; we don't give up on our goal, even when it hurts us to run towards it. An undivided heart is not soft, pink romantic snuggliness. It's a fierce, focused, even suffering heart, which looks towards its one redeemer. A heart which longs and thirsts and waits.

Much of life is waiting as we, from our tick-tock passing of time perspective, don't understand each tick and tock of the world around us. Sometimes they sound so tinny and unimportant; at other times, each tock feels like a miniature death. But in the longing and in the expression of longing we can learn what it is to be undivided, to understand the value of unrelenting love beyond our circumstances and perceptions, even in the midst of suffering. We look for God's kingdom to come, fully, once and for all.

Lord of my heart,
keep me in a constant state of wonder.
Open my eyes to your glory
that I might understand more fully
your importance in my life;
especially when my mind is scattered,
my soul crushed, my heart divided.
When my hands are grubby
with sin and shame,
when my eyes are dimmed
with tiredness and tears,
when I am beyond myself,
utterly unable to save myself
or shine any light of my own,
Holy Spirit, divine breath,

sharp and clear and uncompromising,
blaze through my soul,
burn up all the rubbish
I have allowed to accumulate
until there is nothing to look at but you,
the bright burning presence of God.
May I recognise your beauty
and your power in my life.

REFLECT
- How has this book challenged you?
- What insights do you want to take away?
- How might you put them into practice in your life?

Acknowledgements

... whatever you do, in word or deed,
do everything in the name of the Lord Jesus,
giving thanks to God the Father through him.
Colossians 3:17

If you're family or friend, consider yourself
loved and appreciated.
I do just want to thank some people who have
helped me in the writing of this book:

J and Lizzie, who delight me just by walking into the room
(sorry for hugging you so often).
Thribbiel/Golf Ball Head/Sarah, for the ultimate in
excessive-sharing-by-text-message.
Annie, Lori and Emma – talented writers and my fellow 'goup' girls.
Bev, to whom I owe several Skype sessions after
disappearing down the book-writing rabbit hole
(I thought you'd appreciate a rabbit reference).
CBC – such a wonderful, supportive church family.
Conrad, for general kindred-type-ness and support.
All of 'Lucy's Little Helpers' – you have
exceptional cheerleading skills.
The team at DLT, for daring to publish me again – *thank you.*
Margaret and Mike, for all your encouragement.
Debbie, for supporting me, buying me coffee and letting me talk
incessantly – I wish we could do it more often!
Mum and Dad, for who you are, always.
Andy, for enduring life with a writer, loving me and
buying me lots of cake.
I should probably stop eating cake now.
Well, maybe just one more... to celebrate.